The Cocktailian Chronicles

The Cocktailian Chronicles
Life with The Professor

Volume I

by gaz regan

Illustrated by Stuffy Shmitt

MIXELLANY

"This book is dedicated to everyone on the planet.
No exceptions." gaz regan
(Yes, I stole that from a bumper sticker.)

Mixellany books may be purchased for educational, business, or sales promotional use. For information, please write to Mixellany Limited, 3 Eyford Cottages, Upper Slaughter, Cheltenham, Gloucestershire GL54 2JL United Kingdom. or email jared@mixellany.com

First edition

ISBN 13: 978-1-907434-15-0

British Library Cataloguing in Publication Data.

A catalogue record for this book is available from the British Library.

Contents

Acknowledgements

Thanks for making this boy's dreams come true by helping me get a voice in **The San Francisco Chronicle** go to Diane Teitelbaum and Michael Bauer—read the intro for info on these two. And thanks also to Linda Murphy, my first editor there, and the woman who dealt with the stuff you're about to encounter. Other people at the Chron had a hand in editing my stuff back then, too, and I'm not sure who they were, but Sonia Fuentes was definitely one of the people who helped make my columns better. Thanks, then, to Sonia, and to all the others who touched my work there.

I've called on my buddy Stuffy Shmitt many times over the years to illustrate all sorts of crap that I've come up with, and none of it amounted to anything until this project, so thanks, Stuff, for putting up with my stuff. You've added tons of flavor to this particular cocktail.

And before I sign off, I'll send hugs and kisses to the people of San Francisco who have supported me so well since 2003 when my cocktailian column was launched.

With a hug and a tiny little kiss on the cheek, close to the ear but not too close, if you know what I mean.

gaz regan

Introduction

I met Diane Teitelbaum, wine writer, consultant, educator, and very well respected maven, on a press trip to Portugal. I had no right being on the trip since I'm a hard-liquor-and-cocktails sort of a guy. And although I do love a drop of port every now and again, fortified wines, are not my subject of expertise. It was a fun trip, though. I tried to educate the wine people as much as possible. "It's okay to swallow the stuff," I kept telling them, but it was to no avail. They all just shook their heads and rolled their eyes at me.

Two years or so later I got an email from Diane telling me that the *San Francisco Chronicle* was looking for someone to cover spirits for them, and she gave me the name and email address of her contact there, Michael Bauer. At that point in my career I was a little bored with writing articles that extolled the beauties of the whisky that's distilled in the oldest stills in all Scotland, or the vodka made with water melted from Arctic glaciers, or tequila aged in used port-pipes, hence the faint pink hue, or, well, you get the picture, right? I took my chances then, and penned an email to Mr. Bauer, proposing that I could write about a different cocktail in each column, and that I'd educate the readers about the ingredients in each as I went along. He went for it. I was in hog heaven. I got a regular gig with the *San Francisco Chronicle*. I could hardly believe my luck. If only my high-school English teacher could see me now, I thought. Thanks, Diane. Thanks, Michael.

The column was due to begin in January, 2003, and I planned to call it *The Cocktailian* since that word, now commonplace, was starting to be bandied about at the time—I had sort of a hand in promoting it, but that's a whole other story. The Margarita, I thought, would be a good topic for the first column. That would give me the chance to discuss what kind of tequila works best in the drink, and also to point out that, if you use a product such as Grand Marnier instead of Cointreau, a far drier liqueur, you need to increase the amount of fresh lime juice in the drink so as to balance the sweetness properly.

In late December, 2002, I met up with my bestest friend, Stuffy Shmitt, illustrator of the book you now hold in your hands, in Manhattan. We toured a few bars together, getting into the Christmas spirit, as it were. We were in the Cedar Tavern, I believe, when I boasted to Stuffy of my new gig with the Chron.

"Do us all a favor, then," Stuffy said, "Write something different. Invent a bartender, and a bar, and have him talk to customers. Tell us a story."

The Professor was born that night. I didn't tell the people at the Chron about him. I just penned my first column, used The Professor, my fictitious bartender, and as the vehicle for the Margarita story, and sent it in. I added a note saying that I was very willing to re-write it if they didn't approve—I wasn't willing to lose this gig so quickly, after all—but the column was accepted and printed, so The Professor was destined to stick around for a while.

Lots of people thought that The Professor was based on me, but that was only rarely the case. The Professor was the bartender I wish I could have been. He was far quicker on his feet than I ever was, had snappier, wittier answers for near-as-damn-it everything than I ever had, and although he came unstuck every now and again, for the most part The Professor was a source of knowledge and wisdom on all fronts. I had the luxury of making up everything The Professor had to deal with, and the time to think of answers and witticisms for him to spout. He was always putting one over on his boss, and he always had the last word with his customers. I was not that sort of bartender. Ask around.

I did have a mental picture of The Professor, of course, and I saw him as being an Irish American in his late fifties with white hair and a white beard. He had a ruddy complexion, stood about six-foot two, and he sported a medium-sized beer belly. The Professor worked in a neighborhood bar—that part was based on my career since I never worked in any swank joints— and he liked to have a good time at work. That fits me, too.

As time went by I introduced various regular customers, and people who popped in to The Professor's bar just once, or maybe twice, and although lots of them were based on people I know, some were composite characters. Doc, the guy who spent most afternoons reading a book at the end of The Professor's bar, was one. I had much fun over the four-plus years of the life of

The Professor, and I gave him a great retirement gift when I sent him to Peru where he disappeared in the Urubamba Valley—the Sacred Valley of the Incas. That's the retirement of my dreams. Providing I can get WiFi and Netflix, of course.

The stories in this book are not verbatim the same tales that appeared in the *Chronicle*. Those were edited by the staff at the newspaper before they were published. In this book you'll find the same stories, but this time they've been edited by the fabulous Martha Schueneman, a good friend and a fine editor, indeed. It was far easier to turn over my files for Martha to edit than it would have been to track down the columns as they appeared in the Chron.

In the "A Word at The End of the Bar," sections that follow each piece I'll let you in on which new characters were based on which real people, and I'll give you some background information about what inspired the stuff that goes down at The Professor's bar. And Stuffy Shmitt, the guy who planted the seed from which The Professor grew, has provided the artwork for this book. I think you're gonna love Stuffy's stuff. His Professor doesn't look like the guy in my imagination, and that's been part of the fun of this project—I'm the writer, and I write in my own way, and

Stuffy's the illustrator, so he gets to depict The Professor however he wants

I think I've set you up, then, for the first story, so turn the page and you'll see how The Professor handled his very first customer—the poor sod who made the mistake of ordering a Margarita from him.

Love, Peace, and All That Stuff, gaz regan

P.S. Check out Stuffy's web site at www.stuffyshmitt. com.

Episode I

The Margarita

A cocktailian behind the bar is akin to a saucier in a great restaurant—he or she knows classic recipes back to front, is aware of the flavors in each ingredient, and isn't afraid to alter recipes a little in order to put a little soul into whatever he or she is making. The fictional bartender in this column, known to his friends as "Professor," is a true cocktailian. He offers his customers choices of different brands of spirits and liqueurs, explaining what each ingredient brings to the party, and he strives for perfect balance in every drink he makes. The world needs more cocktailian bartenders.

"You want a Margarita? You've picked a difficult drink." The customer pauses. In most joints ordering a Margarita is an uncomplicated affair, but today he has bellied up to a stretch of mahogany with The Professor at the helm. What can be so difficult about making a Margarita?

First off, he's told, he must choose a tequila. Does he prefer white (*blanco*) tequila—the style that spends no time whatsoever in oak barrels and has a sharp, peppery, vegetal kick? Or is *reposado*, or "rested," tequila more his style? This one spends at least a couple of months in oak, and The Professor tells him that, depending on the brand, these tequilas can make a great base for a Margarita—just as long as they haven't lost their bite.

"What about gold tequila?"

Eyes roll behind the bar. "You don't want gold tequila. You don't want it in a Margarita, you don't want it neat, and you don't want it in your house. Most of that color is just that—color. Gold tequila is way too sweet to make a decent drink. And if you're going to suggest an aged tequila, one that spends at least twelve months in the wood, I'm going to tell you you're in the wrong bar—*añejos* are for after dinner. Sip 'em and savor 'em, but don't put an *añejo* tequila anywhere near a cocktail shaker."

"I think I'd better have a beer while we discuss this." The customer is getting the hang of things. "So I suppose I'm going to go for white or *reposado*?"

"Now you're talking. You need the sharp stuff to make a decent Margarita. And since you're obviously a man of taste, I presume you want a 100-percent agave bottling, right?"

The customer sips his brew. He's heard this phrase before. He knows it's a quality thing, but he's not quite sure what it means. The man behind the stick picks up on this. "See, if it doesn't say 100-percent agave, it's made with *mostly* agave, but they use sugar, too, to get more bulk. It's almost like mixing rum and tequila together. Amateur stuff."

"And agave is . . ."

"It's a plant. Looks like a gigantic pineapple—you can barely get your arms around some of them. Takes about a decade for agaves to get through adolescence, then they get their spikes chopped off before they're roasted, fermented, and distilled. Amaryllis family, you know."

"Well, no, I didn't know that, but you've convinced me—give me a Margarita made with a 100-percent-agave bottling of your finest white or *reposado* tequila—your choice—please." The customer slugs back the rest of his beer.

"Okay, the best in the house are Chinaco, Don Julio, El Tesoro, and Herradura—all top-shelf stuff. And Cuervo makes a dynamite *reposado* tequila called Tradicional. That one works real

well in a Margarita, too. I'll decide on the tequila while you think about whether you want Cointreau or Grand Marnier."

"Another beer while I mull, please."

"See, your second ingredient is an orange liqueur. You can go for a cheap bottle of generic triple sec, but most of them are way too low in alcohol, and really sweet—you don't want to ruin your great tequila with one of those. Cointreau is a triple sec—a bit on the expensive side, but it's dry as a bone, and comes in at a healthy 40-percent alcohol by volume. Grand Marnier comes with the same amount of the good stuff, but it's made from cognac, and it's sweeter than Cointreau."

"Your choice, maestro."

"Tell you what, my shift ends in about twenty minutes, and the boss won't be back for a couple of hours. I'll make us a couple of Margaritas, one with Cointreau, the other with Grand Marnier. You choose your favorite, and I'll do you the favor of drinking the other. Okay?"

"Am I going to need another beer?"

"Nope. Third ingredient is fresh lime juice. No choice there. Gotta be fresh. Gotta be lime."

The customer watches as the bartender goes to work. Tequila flows over the ice in two separate shakers. Lots of tequila.

Orange comes next—Cointreau in one, Grand Marnier in the other—same amount in both. Now comes the lime juice. The barkeep pours about half as much juice into the shaker with Cointreau as he uses in the Grand Marnier version. He catches the customer watching. "You've got to balance out that sweetness in the Grand Marnier unless you want a kiddie drink. Salt or no salt?" There had to be another question. "Tell you what, I'll salt half of each glass rim, and let you decide which you like best."

The customer expects The Professor to dip the glasses into saucers full of Kosher salt, but no. He moistens half of each glass rim with a lime wedge, then rolls just the outer edge of the rim in the salt. "You don't want salt *in* the drink, now, do you?"

The drinks arrive. The customer takes a sip out of each, first with no salt, then from the other side of the glass. "Grand Marnier, no salt. That's my fave."

"I was hoping you'd say that." The Professor picks up the Cointreau version and walks down to the other end of the bar where one of his regulars has been watching the scene. "The usual?"

"Yep."

No inquisition required.

The Margarita

90 ml (3 oz) 100% agave white or *reposado* tequila
60 ml (2 oz) Cointreau or Grand Marnier
30 ml (1 oz) fresh lime juice, if using Cointreau
or
45 ml (1.5 oz) fresh lime juice, if using Grand Marnier
Kosher salt (optional)
Shake all of the ingredients over ice for 10 to 15 seconds.
Strain into a chilled, salt-rimmed (optional) cocktail glass.

A Word at the End of the Bar

I always drank when I worked behind the bar, so I thought it best to let The Professor have a drink in the very first column, just to set the precedent. I've also altered the recipe, too, since I called for too much lime juice in the Grand Marnier version when I first wrote this piece.

Episode 2

The Dreamy Dorini
Smoking Martini

This week, The Professor, our cocktailian bartender, learns that when presented with an unusual cocktail recipe that defies most of the rules of classic mixology, he should not judge a drink by its ingredients. And therein lies a tale.

The Professor rang the old ship's bell to signal the beginning of class, and the four other bartenders sitting across the mahogany stopped gossiping about who went home with whom at their various bars last night, and settled down, ready for their lesson. They gathered at the bar every week at this time—business was slow on Tuesday afternoons—to swap recipes, talk about recently released bottlings of various spirits and liqueurs, and try a few new drinks. This was a bevy of serious bartenders, and each of them had something to add to almost every lesson. Nobody was the teacher here—the object of the class was to listen and learn from everyone who was passionate enough to be involved in the group.

"Okay," said Robert, who ran one of the best cocktail bars in the city. "I've got a doozy of a new drink for us to try this week. It's called the Dreamy Dorini Smoking Martini." A collective groan issued forth from the group. "If you think the name's weird, wait till you get a load of the ingredients—vodka, Laphroaig single malt scotch, and Pernod."

"My God. That sounds awful." The Professor was speaking. "Who the heck thought of this one?" Turned out that the drink was the brainchild of one Audrey Saunders, Director of

Beverages at New York's Carlyle Hotel, where the famous Bemelmans Bar boasted Bobby Short tickling the ivories on a regular basis. Audrey is known in cocktailian circles as the Libation Goddess. "I've heard great things about Libation Goddess's drinks, but I think she might have stuck her neck out too far on this one. Let me see that recipe."

The recipe called for two ounces of vodka, and since it's mixed with a very powerful single malt scotch, the assembled mass agreed that, although they'd stick to a fairly high-end bottling, the brand didn't much matter in this cocktail, just as long as the vodka had a sturdy body. (You can pretty much count on that if you don't buy the cheapest brands.) Now what about the scotch?

The Professor poured a half ounce of the 10-year-old Laphroaig into a shot glass, and by dipping the end of a short straw into the glass, and then placing his finger on the top of the straw, he captured a few drops of scotch and drizzled it over his tongue. The glass was passed through the bartenders, each of them mimicking The Professor until everyone had sampled the whisky.

"My, but that's a powerful dram—peppery, smoky, oily, and intense," said Jen. Jen was a relative newcomer to the group—she worked at a neighborhood joint, but had aspirations of improving her skills and getting a job in a tonier cocktail lounge. She was in the right place. "If this drink works, we could try it with Ardbeg or Lagavulin—they're heavily peated, incredibly smoky malts from the isle of Islay, too. We might even try it with Talisker, from Skye." She paused, running through some other scotches that were stored neatly in her taste memory. "I don't think that Bowmore will be quite smoky enough for this drink, but I know from experience that it makes a dynamite Rob Roy."

The bartenders tasted the Pernod—fairly sweet, and intense with anise flavors, just like most absinthe substitutes. General discussion agreed that they might want to experiment with other bottlings such as Herbsaint or Ricard, but Absente might not be sweet enough to achieve the balance that Saunders envisioned. "You gotta be really careful with this stuff—a tad too much and it can control the whole drink. This recipe calls for only two or three drops, but if you keep some Pernod in a bitters bottle, you can be precise when fixing drinks such as this one," said The Professor. He kept an array of old bitters bottles behind the bar, each one filled with highly-flavored liqueurs such as Pernod, Bénédictine, Chartreuse, and the like.

"Enough talking, let's taste this drink," said John. The bartender on duty went to work, while John told the crowd about Saunders' thoughts on this concoction. "She sees the vodka in the drink as a blank canvas that she 'paints' with the scotch and Pernod."

"It's also going to act as a diluting agent in this drink—soothe the soul of that malt a little," Jen pointed out.

The drink was divine. Sure enough, the vodka did its job. It didn't put the Laphroaig to sleep, but it thoroughly calmed the storm in the whisky; the sweet anise flavors of the Pernod made a perfect foil for the scotch, adding an extra dimension to the cocktail and mingling perfectly with the iodine flavors in the Scottish nectar. The group insisted on trying different versions of the cocktail using the scotches that Jen had suggested, and they all worked fairly well, but Laphroig and Ardbeg—the most intense whiskies of the group—won the day for this recipe. "I've seen grown men cry when I use single malts in mixed drinks," The Professor told the crowd, "but most of these whiskies have so much more character than their blended cousins, they're perfect for the cocktail shaker." The group agreed—they always used top-quality ingredients: "Garbage in. Garbage out," they chanted in unison. It was one of their many mottos.

The Dreamy Dorini Smoking Martini

60 ml (2 oz) vodka
15 ml (.5 oz) Laphroaig 10-year-old single malt scotch
2 to 3 drops Pernod
1 lemon twist, as garnish
Stir all of the ingredients over ice for 20 to 30 seconds.
Strain into a chilled cocktail glass, and add the garnish.

A Word at the End of the Bar

When Audrey first emailed me the recipe for this drink I sent back a one-sentence reply that said something akin to "You're fuckin' crazy." She fired back with "Have you tried the damned drink?" and she was right. I hadn't tried it. And when I did, I realized that Audrey is not just good at what she does, she's God-damned genius. For the record, Audrey says, "I've always liked to use Belvedere [vodka] in The Dreamy Dorini. I think its smooth character provides a nice platform which allows the Laphroaig 10 to shine."

I edited this story just a little, because after it ran in the Chron I got email from a reader informing me that the correct terminology is "tickling the ivories," and I'd originally written "tinkling the ivories." Duh . . . And in case you're wondering, in my mind's eye, the guy called Robert in this story was Robert "DrinkBoy" Hess.

Episode 3

The Pisco Sour

This week our cocktailian bartender, The Professor, gets the chance to dance behind the bar when he introduces one of his regular customers to the delights of the Pisco Sour, a drink reportedly created in 1915 by Victor Morris, an American bartender from Berkeley who owned the Morris Bar in Lima, Peru.

The lunch rush had ended and just one person remained at the bar, a pretty eccentric guy known only as "Doc" to the regulars. Most people believed that Doc was independently wealthy—he spent most afternoons at the bar with his nose buried in old books, sipping whatever took his fancy. There was no "usual" drink for this guy.

"Could you whip me up a Button Punch, Professor?"

"Now that's a tall order, Doc. The recipe for that drink is lost to history. You reading Kipling?"

Indeed, Doc was reading *From Sea to Sea*, Rudyard Kipling's 1899 account of his world travels, in which San Francisco was one of his ports of call: "In the heart of the business quarter, where banks and bankers are thickest, and telegraph wires most numerous, stands a semi-subterranean bar tended by a German with long blond locks and a crystalline eye. Go thither softly, treading on the tips of your toes, and ask him for a Button Punch. 'Twill take ten minutes to brew, but the result is the highest and noblest product of the age. No man knows what is in it. I have a theory it is compounded of the shavings of cherubs' wings, the glory of a tropical dawn, the red clouds of sunset, and fragments of lost epics by dead masters. But try for yourselves, and pause a while to bless me, who am always mindful of the truest interests of my brethren," he wrote.

"Most people agree that Button Punch probably had a pisco-brandy base—pisco was very big in this city in the late 1800s. I can make you a Pisco Sour if you'd like."

"And what would that be, good sir?"

The Pisco Sour was one of The Professor's very favorite drinks. It was the only cocktail he could think of that called for Angostura bitters, not as an actual ingredient, but as an aromatic garnish, dashed on top of the cocktail after it had been shaken and strained. Pisco brandy takes its name from the Peruvian port where it is thought to have been created; it is distilled from a

muscat wine and then is rested for a short time in clay pots before being bottled. Although pisco is also produced in other South American countries, Peruvian bottlings are usually favored by aficionados.

"First you should know that the Pisco Sour gets raw egg white, so if you're afraid of eggs, you won't want to risk this one."

"Eggs don't scare me, Professor, carry on."

"It's a pretty simple affair, really, but pisco brandy is unique—it's colorless, like vodka, and has a sharp, pungent, some-what smoky note that some people compare to scotch. Mix it with fresh lemon juice, simple syrup, and the white of an egg—you have to shake all heck out of this drink to integrate the egg white—and you end up with a silky-textured drink like you've never experienced before."

Now The Professor had to decide which bottling of pis-co brandy to use—he had three on the backbar: Pisco Especial, a fairly simple spirit; Pisco Don Cesar Puro, a sharp, tangy brandy; and Pisco Italia, a smooth pisco that is sometimes sipped neat. Don Cesar was his very favorite for cocktails, though—it gave drinks a nice sharp edge—so choosing was fairly easy. Regina, the sharp-tongued waitress who had been eavesdropping on the conversation, made her way back to the kitchen as soon as she heard Doc agree to try the drink, and returned with a raw egg white from the smallest egg she could find. She had seen The Professor make a Pisco Sour before.

After the ingredients were assembled in the shaker, The Professor did his Joe Cocker imitation, dancing around the bar like a madman, his hands holding the shaker tightly and his arms flying in all directions for a good 20 seconds or more, as required to achieve the right consistency. After adding the aromatic garnish, our man behind the bar instructed his customer to inhale as he sipped his Pisco Sour, and Doc complied readily. "If Kipling's Button Punch was anything like this, it's no wonder he compared it to cherubs' wings," he declared. "I feel pretty close to heaven myself right now."

The Pisco Sour

60 ml (2 oz) pisco brandy
30 ml (1 oz) fresh lemon juice
15 ml (.5 oz) simple syrup
1 raw egg white, from a small egg
Angostura bitters, as an aromatic garnish
Shake vigorously and strain into a chilled champagne flute.
Dash some bitters on top.

A Word at the End of the Bar

Lots of people thought that Doc, the character who gets introduced in this story, was based on Ted "Dr. Cocktail" Haigh, but that's not the case. The Doc who frequented The Professor's bar was 100 percent fictional. I created him to be a foil for The Professor, made him old and a little crusty, just so I could have fun with him, and I made him an avid reader so that I could introduce books through him if need be. I added a little more history about the Pisco Sour in this story, simply because I now know more about the drink's history than I did in 2003. Thanks to my good friend, Diego Loret de Mola, for this added info. And I've also learned that, according to the aforementioned Ted "Dr. Cocktail" Haigh, Button Punch was not a pisco-based concoction at all. It was made with Batavia Arrack, a style of rum that hails from the Island of Java. According to www.alpenz.com, the web site that offers Batavia Arrack van Oosten for sale, Batavia Arrack is "distilled from sugarcane and fermented red rice, using Chinese pot stills with characteristic teak vats." Both Haigh and

Eric Seed, owner of alpenz.com, are upstanding gents, so I'll believe both of them on these details.

These days The Professor would "dry shake" his Pisco Sour initially, or shake it without ice, to better emulsify the egg white, but nobody was doing that in 2003 when I penned this. The "Joe Cocker" shake, by the way, is how I think I look when I shake a drink. The words graceful and gaz have never appeared in the same sentence before this one.

The Red Delicious
& The Chaya Candy Apple Cosmo

This week, The Professor, our cocktailian bartender, makes a couple of tempting drinks created at San Francisco's Chaya Brasserie. And he learns that they can lead to matrimony.

Only an hour to go until closing time, and The Professor was feeling a tad grumpy—night shifts weren't his style anymore, but he was doing another bartender a favor by filling in. The bar-room door opened, and in walked a youngish couple who were far too cheerful for The Professor's liking:

"He'll have a draft beer, and could you make me an Apple Martini like the ones they make at Chaya Brasserie?" asked the woman, flashing a grin that made our cocktailian bartender feel a little better.

"Which one?" he asked.

The customer looked a little puzzled, so The Professor told her that, although they make regular Appletinis at Chaya, they also make two specialty apple drinks, both created by Eric Schreiber, Bar Manager since the place opened just over three years ago. He contributed the Chaya Candied Apple Martini, and a more recent addition to the cocktail list, the Red Delicious. Both of these drinks call for the Van Gogh Wild Appel vodka as a base, but the first one uses Licor 43 (sometimes called Cuarenta y Tres) as a sweetening agent, whereas the Red Delicious employs Sour Apple Pucker or Van Gogh's Applefest—both apple-flavored liqueurs—instead. In Spanish Rose, you refer to this as Licor 43…

"They're variations on the Cosmopolitan, but the second rendition is far more intense with apple flavors than the first. How's about I fix you half-measures of each, and you can decide which suits you best."

"Sounds good to me. Which is *your* favorite, though?"

"I lean towards the Candied Apple version—the Cuarenta y Tres adds a nice hint of herbs and vanilla to the mix. The name makes it sound sweet, but Schreiber balances it out nicely with fresh lime juice and a touch of cranberry juice. When I make the Red Delicious, though, I usually choose the Applefest liqueur over the Pucker—it's a little less sweet and captures a truer apple flavor, just like the Wild Appel vodka. Good stuff, you know."

The Professor had been tasting quite a few apple-flavored spirits of late—Laird's Applejack fared well with sweet vermouth in a sort of Manhattan variation, and that company also offers a wonderful 12-year-old apple brandy that he chose to sip neat. He'd also tried quite a few bottlings of calvados—apple brandy made in the Normandy region of France. The younger bottlings were quite true to their fruit, but the apple flavors started to leave the spirit after they spent a decade or so in wood, and surprisingly came back if the brandy was aged for another

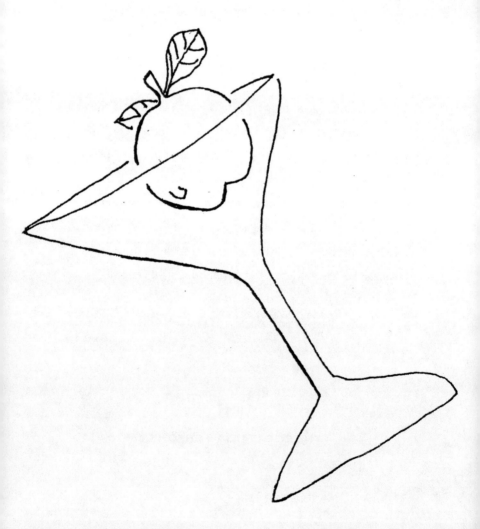

ten years or so. This is a generalization, of course, but it seems to hold true most of the time. The Professor's favorite calvados producers include Daron, Roger Grout, and Christian Drouin.

Van Gogh's Wild Appel vodka, though, knocked The Professor's socks off as a cocktail base. He sometimes merely chilled it over ice and served it straight-up, but that took him away from his what he liked to do best—mix and marry flavors—and he'd come across Schreiber's creations when making his weekly round of San Francisco bars. Sure, he loved to create drinks of his own, but it was also important to see what other bartenders were up to.

Before too long The Professor served the two cocktails to his new friend, and since it was almost time to close, he made a little extra of each for himself.

"Not usually the sort of drink I choose at this hour of the morning—these are so crisp and tart they're beginning to wake me up again," he noted.

"Well the Red Delicious is the one I was sipping at Chaya earlier this evening, and it gave me the courage to propose to this guy right here," said the woman with the winning smile.

"You say yes?" our bartender asked the man in question.

"Sure did. How do you refuse a woman named Eve when she's drinking apples?"

The Red Delicious

45 ml (1.5 oz) Van Gogh Wild Appel vodka
22.5 ml (.75 oz) Van Gogh Applefest
15 ml (.5 oz) fresh lime juice
15 ml (.5 oz) cranberry juice
Shake and strain into a chilled cocktail glass.

The Chaya Candy Apple Cosmo

45 ml (1.5 oz) Van Gogh Wild Appel vodka
15 ml (.5 oz) Licor 43
15 ml (.5 oz) fresh lime juice
15 ml (.5 oz) cranberry juice
Shake and strain into a chilled cocktail glass.

A Word at The End of the Bar

I was quite taken with the Van Gogh Wild Appel vodka when I wrote this piece, and having visited their plant in Holland I can attest to both the quality of their ingredients and the distiller's mastery of his craft. I created another drink using this apple-flavored vodka at around this time, and I made it for Brook Wilkinson, the daughter of my good friends Stephan Wilkinson and Susan Crandell. Here it is.

Pretty in Pink

60 ml (2 oz) Van Gogh Wild Appel vodka

22.5 ml (.75 oz) creme de noyeaux

22.5 ml (.75 oz) fresh lemon juice

Club soda

Shake everything except the club soda over ice and strain into an ice-filled collins glass. Top with club soda (or champagne if you're feeling flush).

The Floridita Cocktail
& The Floridita Daiquiri

This week The Professor, bumps into a guy who's somewhat of a legend in the cocktailian world, and they discuss a couple of drinks created at one of Ernest Hemingway's favorite Cuban bars.

The Professor was not in a good mood. He'd shown up for work at six o'clock in the morning because the boss had decided to make a little extra cash by turning the whole joint over to a movie company for the day. Naturally, The Professor was assigned to supervise. Lights and wires were strung all over the place, and now, some twelve hours later, the crew was just starting to call it a day. There wasn't a penny in the tip cup.

"Don't suppose there's a chance of getting a Floridita Daiquiri to help me wind down, is there?"

The crew member standing at the bar had The Professor's full attention.

"You talking about the one with maraschino liqueur?"

"Yep. Do you need the full recipe?"

The Professor shot him a look. "Straight up or frozen?"

Little did our cocktailian friend know that he was in the presence of none other than Dr. Cocktail, a graphic designer in the movie business who studies the history of cocktails and mixed drinks as a hobby. Born Edward Newman Haigh II, Dr. Cocktail is one of the few authorities on this subject in the world. He requested the straight-up version, and watched as The Professor assembled the drink.

It's key to use a white, sometimes called light, rum in a Floridita Daiquiri—aged products such as amber or *añejo* rums aren't usually sharp enough for the drink—but not just any old white rum was going to suffice for this obviously fussy guy waiting patiently at the mahogany. The Professor perused the rum bottles on the backbar.

"Best white rums in this joint are the Appleton White, Rhum Barbancourt Traditional, or the Brugal White Label. What'll it be?"

"Your choice, Professor."

Our bartender paused—how did this guy know his nickname? He reached for the Appleton bottle. All three of these rums have lots of character and texture—they aren't merely peppery versions of vodka like some of the less expensive bottlings—but The Professor had had a soft spot for Appleton ever since he'd visited Jamaica. (He'd never visited Haiti or the Dominican Republic where Barbancourt and Brugal, respectively, are made.) Adding some fresh lime juice, simple syrup, and a tad of maraschino liqueur to the rum and ice in his shaker, The Professor shook and strained the drink into an ice-cold cocktail glass.

Setting the drink in front of Haigh, The Professor asked: "You ever been to the Floridita bar in Havana?"

"No, I never got the chance. It was known as La Florida back in 1930—I have their recipe booklet from that year. It was Hemingway's favorite haunt unless he wanted a Mojito …"

"That's right—he went over to La Bodeguita for those. Wait a minute—movies, mixed drinks—are you Dr. Cocktail, by any chance?"

"Some call me that. And you, sir, are quite obviously The Professor I've heard about."

The Professor was a happy man again. He'd heard of Haigh, but had never met the man. Dr. Cocktail has a reputation for being free with his information, so our bartender took the opportunity to pick his brain.

"What do you know about the Floridita Cocktail—the one with sweet vermouth?"

"It's a different drink entirely, but not without merit, and not without one slight similarity, too. The maraschino in the Daiquiri you just made is barely detectable, but the almond nuttiness of the liqueur is there all the same—just as it should be. In the Floridita Cocktail it's the chocolate notes of crème de cacao that lurk in the background—they're both astonishingly subtle drinks."

The Professor shook up a Floridita Cocktail and handed it to Haigh. He got a kick out of the satisfied grin that appeared on the Doctor's face after his first sip.

"I didn't spot a single star here today—who's in this flick?"

"She's not in this scene, but would you believe Mariel Hemingway?"

Floridita Daiquiri

60 ml (2 oz) light rum
22.5 ml (.75 oz) fresh lime juice
15 ml (.5 oz) simple syrup
7.5 ml (.25 oz) maraschino liqueur
Shake over ice and strain into a chilled cocktail glass.

Floridita Cocktail

45 ml (1.5 oz) light rum
15 ml (.5 oz) sweet vermouth
15 ml (.5 oz) fresh lime juice
7.5 ml (.25 oz) white crème de cacao
splash of grenadine
Shake over ice and strain into a chilled cocktail glass.

A Word at The End of the Bar

don't have much to add to this one, but I'll once again take the opportunity to thank Ted Haigh for teaching me so damned much about cocktailian history—he's such a generous soul.

Episode 6

The Red Snapper

This week The Professor, our man behind the stick, makes a Bloody Mary in its original form, and discusses a somewhat controversial work of art with a new customer.

Sunday brunch-time is always busy at The Professor's bar, and today is no exception—the tables are full of people eating eggs in various guises and gulping Bloody Marys, each one made according to The Professor's secret formula.

"Let me have Eggs Benedict with extra hollandaise sauce, and could I get a Red Snapper instead of a Bloody Mary?" The question comes from a stranger sitting at the bar who has been perusing the brunch menu for the last few minutes.

"The Red Snapper *is* a Bloody Mary, unless you'd like me to make the drink in its original form—the way they served it at the St. Regis Hotel's King Cole Bar in New York back in the thirties and forties," The Professor offers.

"That's exactly what I'm looking for—a little blast from the past to savor on a Sunday afternoon. A bartender at the King

Cole Bar told me all about the drink when I was back East a couple of weeks ago."

"Did he tell you about the secret of the King Cole mural, too?"

"Yes, he did, but he made me promise not to spill the beans."

"That's right—you hear it at their bar or not at all."

The mural in question was painted by Maxfield Parrish at the turn of the twentieth century after Parrish boasted that he could paint any subject under the sun. At first glance, it's a jolly rendering of King Cole on his throne, surrounded by courtiers and jesters, but once you hear about the true subject of the painting, the mural never looks the same again.

The Bloody Mary was created by Frenchman Fernand "Pete" Petiot, who held forth from behind the stick at Harry's New York Bar in Paris in the 1920s. The drink was reputedly introduced to the United States when John Astor, then owner of the St. Regis, lured Petiot to New York in 1934. The name was changed to the Red Snapper for at least a decade, until Astor decided that the public could probably cope with the name, *Bloody Mary*.

"Any particular vodka in mind?" The Professor waits as the stranger peruses the vodka collection on the backbar.

"You have a suggestion?"

"Unless you're drinking vodka neat, or perhaps in a very dry Vodka Martini, I don't think it matters too much, but you might want to try one of the newer bottlings that hit the shelves recently. We have Ciroc, Citadelle, and Vertical, all from France—the Vertical is made by monks—and a couple of great California vodkas, Hangar One and Domain Charbay. There's also Türi, an Estonian vodka that's starting to get a pretty big following. Want me to go on? They're all top-notch."

"No, sir, just pick one and mix away, if you please."

The Professor fills the mixing glass with ice and pours in as much vodka as tomato juice before adding a little lemon juice and one or two spices. He then pours the contents of the glass into the metal half of the shaker, reverses the procedure, and pours back and forth about a half-dozen times before he strains it into a chilled cocktail glass. The stranger eyes him curiously.

"It's a method I picked up from Dale "King Cocktail" De-Groff when he used to work the Rainbow Room in Manhattan," says The Professor. "This way the juice doesn't get too aerated."

"And your recipe?"

"Straight from Gaston Lauryssen, manager of the St. Regis Hotel in the forties—it was published in the 1945 book, *Crosby Gaige's Cocktail Guide and Ladies' Companion*.

Patrick, a regular customer at The Professor's joint, has been eavesdropping on the conversation. "What's the secret behind that darned mural? I've seen it, but didn't know I should have asked about it."

The stranger leans into Patrick cautiously, "Since you've seen it I'll tell you, but don't let anyone at the St. Regis get wind of it..."

The Red Snapper

60 ml (2 oz) tomato juice
60 ml (2 oz) vodka
1/2 teaspoon Worcestershire sauce
1 pinch salt
1 pinch cayenne pepper
1 dash fresh lemon juice
Pour into an ice-filled mixing glass; transfer into a metal shaker, and reverse the process several times to incorporate the ingredients. Strain into a chilled cocktail glass.

A Word at The End of the Bar

I n 2007 *The New York Times* published an article about the King Cole mural, and in it they spilled the beans about its secret. I found this article in seconds flat by using a decent search engine to look for "King Cole Mural," so now that the cat's out of the bag—and that's a damned shame—I won't leave you hanging lest you don't know about this. In the words of Glenn Collins, who penned the piece for the Times: "The legend, repeated by generations of bar patrons, is that the king's sheepish grin, and the startled reactions of his knights, were occasioned by the flatulence of the monarch."

Collins' article also revealed that the Astor who commissioned the mural was, in fact, John Jacob Astor IV, and rumor has it that he asked Parrish to make the King to look like him, so if you ever see this piece of art, you'll presumably know exactly what John Jacob Astor IV looked like when he broke wind. How very lovely, huh?

Episode 7

The Tangier Tartini

This week The Professor tunes in to flavored vodkas, grumbles about his penny-pinching boss, and makes a cocktail developed at Aziza restaurant on Geary Boulevard.

Half an hour to go until opening time. The Professor is cutting his fruit garnishes, making sure that he gets a maximum of six wedges from any lime or lemon, despite the fact that the Boss has told him over and over again that fruit is expensive and garnishes should be small. Inside his head, The Professor recalls one of many discussions on this subject.

"You can't serve a Gin and Tonic with a sliver of lime— you gotta squeeze some juice into that drink before it's served."

"Yeah, well, squeeze a couple o' drops from a tenth of a lime, then."

"Sure, Boss."

The door opens and a delivery guy walks in with a couple of cases of liquor on his hand-truck.

"Watcha got there?" The Professor enquires.

"Half-a-dozen each of the Charbay flavored vodkas."

"Great. Let me have one of each for behind the bar, and stick the rest at the very back of the storeroom before the grouch sees what I ordered—he always wants me to buy the cheap stuff. Doesn't realize that these aren't *very* pricey, and I can get an extra 50 cents to a buck for every cocktail I make with them."

Located in St. Helena in the Napa Valley, the Domaine Charbay distillery is run by Miles Karakasevic with the help of his wife Susan, son Marko, and daughter Lara. Miles is a twelfth-generation master distiller from Europe, and Marko is currently apprenticing under him. It was Marko who convinced his father to start making fruit-flavored vodkas in 1998.

The Professor opens the door at 11:30 a.m. sharp and deals with the lunch customers for a couple of hours. Now the bar is quiet again, and just two guys remain—both bartenders at local joints enjoying their day off by coming to see our man behind the stick.

"Anything new for us to sample, Professor?" asks Jonathan, an up-and-coming cocktailian who recently arrived in San Francisco from New York.

"Yeah, I finally got the Charbay flavored vodkas in, though the Boss doesn't know it yet. Let's have some fun."

The Professor pours samples of all four bottlings into small glasses, and the three bartenders take turns in inhaling, then sipping, each one. Ruby Red Grapefruit, Key Lime, Meyer Lemon, and Blood Orange—each is true to the flavor of the real fruit.

"These guys really know what they're doing—I took their distillery tour a couple of weeks ago," says Jonathan. "They use whole fruits to make an extract—Marko calls it an 'ancient Serbian extract technique,' but he wears a grin as he says it—then they marry the extract with their unflavored vodka and bottle it at 80-proof. Great stuff."

Jeff, the other bartender, is older than Jonathan, but he keeps up on current trends. He pulls a crumpled piece of paper from his pocket, opens it up, and says, "Let's make a Tangier Tartini."

"Beg pardon?" says Jonathan.

"I bumped into Farnoush Deylamian from Aziza restaurant last night—she gave me a recipe for one of the Charbay cocktails she created for her place. They got belly dancers there, too."

"Calm down, Jeff," The Professor admonishes, "Let's have a look at that recipe."

"Farnoush came up with the name because Tangiers is where lots of tropical fruits are shipped from—grapefruit and guava included. She uses fresh guava nectar, too—for a general manager Farnoush is quite a cocktailian."

The Professor makes a Tangier Tartini, and is straining it into a chilled cocktail glass when the door opens and the Boss walks in.

"Giving the store away again, Professor?"

"Right, Boss, but don't worry, I'm using only the best stuff."

The Tangier Tartini

60 ml (2 oz) Charbay Ruby Red Grapefruit vodka
30 ml (1 oz) guava nectar
7.5 ml (.25 oz) simple syrup
15 ml (.5 oz) tonic water
Mango slice with peel, as garnish
Shake the vodka, guava nectar, and simple syrup over ice. Strain into a chilled cocktail glass, top with the tonic, and add the garnish.

A Word at the End of the Bar

've had a long relationship with the guys at Charbay, and not only are their products startlingly fabulous, the whole Karakasevic family has been very warm to me over the years. My favorite story about Miles Karakasevic, the patriarch, goes back to the late 1990s. Mardee and I were providing spirits reviews for the *Wine Enthusiast* magazine, and producers were sending samples to us right, left, and center. I interviewed Miles during this period for some article or other, and I mentioned to him that, should he want any of his products to be reviewed in the mag, we'd be only too happy to do that, if he just sent a sample.

"You want my spirits, you buy my spirits," he told me in his thick Eastern European accent. I loved him from that moment on!

Jonathan and Jeff, the two bartenders in this piece, were based on Jonathan Pogash, "The Cocktail Guru," and his father, my dear old friend Jeff Pogash, who works for Moet-Hennessy USA in Manhattan.

Episode 8

Mahogany

The Professor is wearing a baffled look on his otherwise wizened face—Doc, a regular customer who always has his nose buried in a book, has just ordered a Tailspin cocktail, and our bartender doesn't know how to make it.

"Did you just make that one up? I can't recall ever hearing of it."

"Excuse me, but no, he didn't. Here's the recipe."

The Professor's head turns toward the tall stranger sitting at the bar who is offering up his PDA. He takes a look, and sure enough, a recipe for the Tailspin is right there on the screen—equal parts gin, sweet vermouth, and green Chartreuse, with a dash or two of Campari.

"This is a Bijou with Campari instead of orange bitters," says The Professor, thankful for being able to save face in a small way.

"Correct, sir—not many people know the Tailspin, so I keep the recipe in my Pocket PC in case of emergencies."

"How many other recipes you got in there?"

"Oh, over 4,000 at this point. You never know when you need this sort of thing."

"You a cocktail geek?"

"Actually I'm more of a computer geek, and a cocktail freak. Robert Hess." The stranger holds out his hand, and The Professor shakes it with a smile on his face. This guy is a kindred spirit.

"They call me Professor. Pleased to meet you, Robert. Any other obscure recipes I should know about in there?"

"There's one you probably won't know about since I created it just a few months ago. It's called Mahogany—two parts dry vermouth, and one part each of Jägermeister and Bénédictine."

"Sounds weird."

"It *is* weird. Works, though."

The Professor serves the Tailspin he's been making to Doc, and pauses to think about the ingredients in the Mahogany . Jägermeister is a German herbal liqueur that some folk think tastes like cough medicine, and Bénédictine is another herbal liqueur—somewhat sweeter, more honeyed. Both these ingredients are very bold, and either one can easily take over a cocktail

if not used sparingly. "What on earth made you put both these liqueurs in the Mahogany?"

"A German guy challenged me to find a good cocktail that called for Jäger, but when I looked I found that most drinks that call for it either magnified its taste or attempted to hide it completely, so I decided to see what I could come up with myself. I found that dry vermouth took the edge off the Jäger, but I still needed to round off the medicinal notes, and Bénédictine worked perfectly. I usually coat the interior of the glass with my homemade cinnamon tincture, too—it gives an extra little 'pop' to the drink."

"Gee, I used the last of my cinnamon tincture last night," The Professor says with a roll of his eyes.

"Not a problem." Hess pulls a small atomizer from his pocket and hands it to The Professor. "Consider that yours. When you run out, just rinse the glass with cinnamon schnapps instead. That should do the trick."

The Professor assembles the drink and divides it between two cocktail glasses, both coated with the cinnamon tincture. One goes to Doc, who puts his book down for a minute to try this new drink, and The Professor sips on the other. "Good God, man, this is incredibly good. Welcome, Robert. You're a cocktailian whiz."

"Thanks, Professor. Visit my web site some time: Drink-Boy.com."

"DrinkBoy?"

"Yes—there's a fun side to cocktails, too, you know."

From his end of the bar, Doc interjects, "This book I'm reading is about the original compilation of the *Oxford English Dictionary*. The title seems to suit this discussion perfectly."

"And the title is . . . ?" asks Hess.

"*The Professor and the Madman*."

Mahogany

15 ml (.5 oz) cinnamon schnapps (optional)

45 ml (1.5 oz) dry vermouth

22.5 ml (.75 oz) Jägermeister

22.5 ml (.75 oz) Bénédictine

1. If desired, coat the interior of a chilled cocktail glass with the cinnamon schnapps and discard any excess.

2. Stir the vermouth, Jägermeister, and Bénédictine together over ice. Strain into the cocktail glass.

A Word at the End of the Bar

Robert Hess is, perhaps, the most generous soul in the whole cocktail universe. He's a big-wig at Microsoft, he's been our unpaid webmaster since we first launched the Ardent Spirits site, and he answers emails in seconds flat. Ask around—he doesn't just do this stuff for me.

Thanks, Robert.

Episode 9

The Mint Julep

The Professor senses an argument brewing at the end of the bar and saunters toward the suspected malcontents to eavesdrop.

"It's an aromatic garnish."

"It's a darned ingredient. You should be able to taste the mint in a Julep."

"You 'taste' the mint when you inhale as you're sipping. Remember what Irvin S. Cobb's grandfather said: 'Any guy who'd crush the leaves would put scorpions in a baby's bed.'"

The discussion between John and Jen, both local bartenders, is getting out of control. Jen hasn't spent as much time behind the stick as John, but her quote from early twentieth-century newspaperman Cobb proves she's been researching the Mint Julep in preparation for the Kentucky Derby celebrations on Saturday. The Professor decides to weigh in on the argument.

"The most important things about a Julep are figuring out which whiskey to use and how much simple syrup to add to balance it out," he chimes in.

"What about the ice on the outside of the glass?" asks John, with a smug grin.

"Okay, the ice is important, too, but the mint is just a matter of personal preference. Let's look at some whiskeys before we go any further."

The Professor brings a few bottles of Kentucky bourbon to the end of the bar, and they discuss each one in turn. Maker's Mark, they decide, won't need a great deal of syrup—it has a soft, honeyed body with an underlying fruitiness that's nicely balanced with hints of pepper and leather. Wild Turkey, on the other hand, is a wonderfully gruff soul, especially the 101-proof bottling. Quite a lot of sweetening needed for this one.

"I've never tried this Evan Williams seven-year-old," says Jen.

"It's fairly inexpensive, but really high quality, and although it's not as in-your-face as the Wild Turkey, I don't skimp on the syrup when I use this one in a Julep," notes The Professor. Here's a newish whiskey that I'm dying to use in a Mint Julep: George T. Stagg 15-year-old."

"A 15-year-old in a Julep?" questions John.

"Garbage in. Garbage out," recite Jen and The Professor in unison.

The Stagg bourbon is bottled at barrel strength—137.6-proof—and it's dry as a bone, save for some wonderful dried fruit notes in the backdrop. A fairly hefty dose of syrup will be needed for this bourbon. The last two bottlings the bevy of bartenders discuss are Woodford Reserve, a well-balanced whiskey that leans toward the sweet side but has a hint of old leather that rounds out the experience, and Knob Creek, a big-bodied, fruity bourbon with a touch of spice in the finish. Neither of these whiskeys will need to be heavily sweetened to make a good Mint Julep.

The Professor starts to assemble two Juleps—one with muddled mint and a few sprigs for garnish, the other with just whiskey and simple syrup, but such a large bouquet of mint on top that the mound of crushed ice is completely covered.

"The sheet of ice that appears on the exterior of the glass is easier to achieve in silver Julep cups, but you know how cheap the Boss is ..."

"My boss, too," says John, "but I get ice on a tall collins glass quite easily."

Short straws are added to each glass so that, when the Juleps are sampled, the drinker's nose is buried in the mint. The Juleps are sipped. John likes the version with the muddled mint,

and of course, Jen goes for the glass with the mint as only an aromatic garnish.

"Cobb's grandfather sure knew what he was talking about," offers Jen.

The Professor walks down to the other end of the bar, leaving the duo to duke it out on their own.

"What the heck is going on down there?" asks Regina, the raunchy waitress who tries not to miss anything happening at the bar.

"It's that time of year again: You need the longest of arguments to lead up to the fastest two minutes in sports."

The "Aromatic" Mint Julep

Crushed ice
90 ml (3 oz) bourbon
simple syrup, to taste
8 to 10 stems of fresh mint, as garnish

Cut straws so that they are approximately 2 inches taller than the Julep cup or Collins glass. Add crushed ice until the glass is half-full. Add the bourbon and simple syrup, and stir for 10 to 20 seconds. Add more crushed ice and stir again until a thin layer of ice forms on the outside of the glass. Add still more crushed ice so that it domes slightly over the top of the glass. Garnish with the fresh mint stems, and insert the straws. Serve with a cocktail napkin to catch the condensation.

A Word at the End of the Bar

The full quote from Irvin S. Cobb is, "My grandfather always insisted that a man who would let the crushed leaves and the mangled stemlets steep in the finished decoction would put scorpions in a baby's bed," and it's found in *Irvin S. Cobb's Own Recipe Book,* a book published in 1934 by Frankfort Distilleries. And upon close inspection it becomes apparent that Cobb's grandfather didn't actually object to the mint leaves being crushed, he just liked to fish them out of the drink before serving it. Whatever Cobb's Grandpappy's preferences, I personally like the mint to be an aromatic garnish in a Mint Julep. There's something so damned delightful about the aromas of the mint meeting the sweetened whiskey at the back of the throat, and it's an experience to which we're seldom treated, thus making the first Saturday in May all the more special.

The seven-year-old Evan Williams bourbon mentioned in this piece is no longer available, but the Evan Williams Black Label bourbon is every bit as good, even though it doesn't sport an age statement.

Episode 10

The Copper Swan

The Professor is in trouble. And rightfully so. A salesperson told him about three new bottlings of Bowmore single malt scotch, and he ordered them without even glancing at the price.

"These sell for two grand apiece in the liquor store. How many of our customers are going to spring for a dram of one of these?" yelled the Boss, his face turning bright red as he thought about his money gathering dust on the backbar.

"Let's see, that works out to just under eighty-four bucks an ounce. Suppose I can sell them at, say, $100 an ounce. That gives you around $15 profit per drink, even if you were buying at retail. If I sell 60 shots you'll be making a profit, and we'll still have about a dozen shots left. Hefty profit if I sell them all ..."

"You're a dreamer, Professor. A dreamer ..."

"Set me up a flight of those Bowmores, willya?" The order comes from Doug, an entrepreneur who hangs out at The Professor's bar when his travels bring him to Fog City.

"Three half-ounce pours are gonna set you back one-fifty buckaroos, my good man."

"In that case make it three full ounces. I just closed a huge technology deal in India. And while you're at it, set up another flight for your good self and that grumpy looking guy with the loud voice."

The Professor can't even look at his boss, and he tries to hide his smirk as he assembles the flights of whiskies, one for Doug, his new-found savior, and two sets of half measures for the Boss and himself.

All three bottlings of Bowmore were distilled in 1964; one was aged in a used fino sherry butt, another in an oloroso sherry butt, and the third slumbered in a used bourbon cask—each for over 38 years. What will the trio make of these?

"Fino."

"Fino."

"Fino. One of the most elegant, delicate drams I've ever sampled. Did you get pears and newly mown grass in the nose?" asks Doug.

"Yep, and a real subtle smokiness on the palate. The oloroso bottling was great, too—full of Christmas spices and dark fruits," notes The Professor.

"I enjoyed the bourbon cask whisky—very masculine with leather and tobacco notes. If we weren't tasting it against these other two, I dare say we'd be raving over it." The Boss has calmed down now that he has a little whisky in his system, not to mention the $600 in his register.

"Wanna make me a Copper Swan to round out the afternoon?"

"Sure, Doug. What kind of whisky?"

"Well, the original was made with the Highland Park 12-year-old. How about we step it up to the 18-year-old while I'm still feeling flush?"

Highland Park, made on the isle of Orkney in the Outer Hebrides, is an incredibly well-balanced single malt with salty notes, whiffs of peat, and a very full body. The 12-year-old is delightful, but the 18-year-old, with muted iodine notes followed swiftly by peat, honey, dried cherries, heather, and a great, sharp, lactic note, is one of The Professor's all-time favorite malts. He pours a good measure of whisky into his mixing glass, adds a touch of apricot brandy, and stirs the drink over ice for almost half a minute.

"It's important to mix cocktails long enough for them to chill properly, and so that enough of the ice melts to soothe the soul of the spirits," he explains to Doug, who is drumming his fingers on the bar while he waits.

The Professor strains the cocktail into a chilled champagne flute. "Far easier to handle than those damnable Martini glasses," he says as he releases the oils from a large lemon twist onto the top of the drink and gently rubs the outer rind around the rim of the glass.

Doug takes a sip of his Copper Swan and sighs. "This is as close to Nirvana as I'm going to get," he says.

"Let me take you one step further. This one's on the house." Out of the corner of his eye, The Professor sees the Boss shaking his head in disbelief as he disappears toward the office.

"You just can't resist, can you?"

"No, Doug, I can't. When I'm in the Boss's good books, things just don't seem quite right around here. Wanna try a Rob Roy with this Bowmore fino cask?"

The Copper Swan

45 ml (1.5 oz) Highland Park single malt scotch
22.5 ml (.75 oz) apricot brandy
1 lemon twist, as garnish
Stir all of the ingredients over ice for 20 to 30 seconds.
Strain into a chilled cocktail glass, and add the garnish.

A Word at the End of the Bar

This story is a good example of how different The Professor is from me—I would never have dared treat any of my bosses this way, and that's probably why I gave The Professor such huge balls—I lived vicariously through him, I think.

Doug, the guy who closed a huge tech deal in India in this piece, is a good friend of mine, though I'm letting him keep his anonymity here. Cheers, Doug,

Episode 11

The Phoebe Snow

I t's around four o'clock in the afternoon, and The Professor is cleaning the bar, getting ready for the after-work crowd to arrive. The waitress, Regina, turned up for work wearing a pleated, plaid miniskirt, white knee socks, and a white shirt with a striped tie this morning, and The Professor would have sent her home to change if there had been enough time. The lunch-time regulars seemed to enjoy her attire, though. As The Professor shoots Regina yet another dirty look he sees her eyes light up and turns to see Stuffy walk through the door.

Stuffy is a musician/bartender who often stops in to see The Professor for a quick Irish whiskey before he goes to work.

"Hi Stuffy. Irish?"

"Yeah. Make it a double, I'm broke."

"Might as well not pay me for two as stiff me for one, huh?"

"Something like that."

The Professor sets a whiskey in front of Stuffy and starts to hum a tune from the seventies as he polishes the liquor bottles on the backbar.

"I can name that tune in three notes," says Stuffy

"I wish you would—I can't get it out of my head, but I can't for the life of me remember the title."

"It was a Phoebe Snow song."

"Phoebe Snow. That's right. There's a Phoebe Snow cocktail, you know …"

"I didn't think she was famous enough to have a drink named for her."

"She wasn't."

The Professor explains that the original Phoebe Snow was a fictitious character used by the Lackawanna Railroad to promote their use of anthracite, circa 1900. This "new" form of coal was said to be cleaner than the older, more common bituminous variety, and Phoebe Snow wore a spotless white dress and gloves to prove the point. The cocktail has been around since the early 1900s.

"I won my fame and wide acclaim

For Lackawanna's splendid name

By keeping white and snowy bright

Upon the road of anthracite," chants The Professor.

"Yeah, very catchy, Professor. Okay, fix me a Phoebe Snow, and don't tell a soul I strayed from my Irish."

"That'll be three drinks you owe for. No, make it two. This one's on the house."

The Professor grabs a bottle of Dubonnet Rouge from the backbar and starts to build the drink in an ice-filled mixing glass. Dubonnet is an apéritif wine that's been around since the mid-1800s. It's flavored with quinine and various herbs, fortified with a little brandy, and it's made in rouge and blanc bottlings. Both can be used instead of vermouth in drinks such as Manhattans and Dry Gin Martinis, but it's best to use them judiciously—they have more pronounced flavors than most vermouths.

"What if there's no Dubonnet around, Professor?"

"Then you can't make a Phoebe Snow. You could try using Lillet Rouge,—it's in the same family, but the Lillet is a little more delicate. I make this drink with equal parts of Dubonnet and brandy, but I'd probably use more Lillet if that's all I had."

The Professor looks at the brandies behind the bar and reaches for a bottle of Cardinal Mendoza Solera Gran Reserva Brandy de Jerez, a highly regarded Spanish brandy that's fruity enough to act as a good counterpoint to the quinine in the Dubonnet yet is by no means overly sweet. A few dashes of Pernod, a sweetish anise-flavored liqueur, are added to the mixing glass, and The Professor starts to stir the ingredients together. When he deems that the cocktail is ready, he strains it into a chilled champagne flute.

"No garnish?"

"Not traditionally, but I'll add a twist of lemon if you like."

"No, I think I'll just knock this back before anyone catches me."

Stuffy takes a large swallow of his Phoebe Snow cocktail.

"You're a Poetry Man, Professor."

"Yeah, yeah, but what was the name of that darned song?"

The Phoebe Snow

30 ml (1 oz) brandy
30 ml (1 oz) Dubonnet Rouge
1 to 3 dashes Pernod
Stir over ice and strain into a chilled cocktail glass.

A Word at the End of the Bar

Yep, this story features Stuffy Shmitt, my good buddy and the guy who's providing the artwork for this book. Go check out his music at stuffyshmitt.com—he's pretty damned fabulous.

The Phoebe Snow story always fascinated me. For years, I thought that the drink was named for the singer, and when I saw the recipe in a very old cocktail book I was pretty flabbergasted. When I discovered the story of the original Phoebe Snow—and this was prior to decent search engines coming along—I loved the tale. I also love playing with Dubonnet—it's gotten me out of a jam on many an occasion since it possesses such a sturdy body that is an excellent foil to many strong-flavored ingredients. Here's an extra recipe to prove my point—it's a drink of which I'm fairly proud.

DAM aka Reluctant Tabby Cat

Created for MOTAC'S World Cocktail Day, 2007, New York.

37.5 ml (1.25 oz) Dubonnet Rouge

15 ml (.5 oz) Pallini Limoncello

7.5 ml (.25 oz) Laphroaig 10-year-old single malt scotch

1 lemon twist, as garnish

Shake over ice and strain into a chilled wine goblet. Add the garnish.

Another Word at the End of the Bar

I n 2007, Dale DeGroff, President of the Museum of the American Cocktail, asked me to create a new drink for the Museum's celebration of World Cocktail Day, and he mandated that Laphroaig single malt scotch, a very smoky dram that can be hard to work with when creating cocktails, must be one of the ingredients. It took me the best part of a very frustrating afternoon to find the right ingredients to marry to the Laphroaig, but I must admit that I was pleased with the resultant drink. It won't be everyone's cup of tea, but it went nicely with the barbecued pulled pork with which it was paired at the celebratory dinner that year. The name, "DAM," is an acronym. The letters stand for "Dale's A Man with whom I must have a word," or something like that. A couple of people didn't see the humor in the name, so just to keep them smiling I came up with The Reluctant Tabby Cat as an alternative. Don't ask.

Episode 12

The Bronx Cocktail

The Professor, our cocktailian bartender, is excitedly telling a few of his regular customers about his recent trip to Manhattan, and his visit to the Bull and Bear, the bar in the Waldorf-Astoria Hotel.

"The original bronze sculptures of the bull and bear are right above the bar. They witnessed the birth of the Rob Roy, the Bobbie Burns, and the Bronx Cocktail, and they saw Mark Twain, Buffalo Bill, and Bat Masterson quaffing cocktails way back when the old place was on the site of today's Empire State Building. It was a pretty religious experience," he tells the assembled crowd.

"Don't get carried away, Professor. It's just a bar, you know," admonishes Stephan, a cynical curmudgeon who races on the NASCAR circuit for a living. "And wasn't there once a sculpture of a lamb there, too?"

"Yes, nobody seems to know what became of it. The lamb represented the public, and the story goes that the bartenders surrounded it with flowers saying that that's all that was left for the public after Wall Street's bulls and bears got through with them."

"That's not quite the way I heard it, but the other version shouldn't be told in mixed company," says Stephan. "Now tell us about this Bronx Cocktail. I've never heard of it."

The Professor tells the story of Johnnie Solon, the Waldorf bartender who created the Bronx when he was challenged to make a new drink on the spur of the moment. Solon reportedly called it the Bronx because of his recent visit to the Bronx Zoo: "I saw, of course, a lot of beasts I had never known [and] customers used to tell me of the strange animals they saw after a lot of mixed drinks." When the waiter asked Solon the name of the drink he thought of his trip to the zoo, and told him it was called a Bronx.

As The Professor starts to assemble the drink for Stephan, who has decided to test it so that he might find something else to gripe about, he surveys the gins on the backbar.

"You don't want one of the more traditional 'in-your-face' gins for this drink, so that rules out Beefeater, Junipero, Plymouth, Tanqueray, and Van Gogh. Save these for Dry Gin Martinis, Gin and Tonics, and drinks where you really want the perfumed

aromas of juniper to shine through. In the mid-pungency range we have a new gin that's pretty good, Magellan. It's blue."

"And it's blue because . . . ?"

"Infused with irises. Flower and roots to boot. We have a yellow gin, too—saffron, before you ask—it's called Old Raj, and it's fairly pungent, but leans a little toward the softer side. It's also the most expensive gin we have. Your other choices in medium-perfumed gins are Boodles, Citadelle, or Tanqueray No. 10. If you want a really soft gin, try Bombay or Leyden."

"I drink Tanqueray Martinis, so let me try the Tanqueray No. 10."

Stephan's daughter, Brook, sidles up to the bar.

"And I'll have one made with Old Raj. You're paying, right, Dad?" Stephan shakes his head in disbelief, then gives The Professor a nod. "I'm beginning to feel like that poor lamb from the Waldorf," he says.

"Nothing left in the wallet but flowers, Stephan?"

"I was thinking of the other story, actually. Wait till Brook leaves and I'll fill you in."

The Bronx Cocktail

60 ml (2 oz) gin
7.5 ml (.25 oz) sweet vermouth
7.5 ml (.25 oz) dry vermouth
30 ml (1 oz) fresh orange juice
1 to 2 dashes orange bitters
1 orange twist, as garnish
Shake over ice and strain into a chilled cocktail glass. Add the garnish.

A Word at the End of the Bar

Let's get Stephan and Brook out off the way first: Stephan is based on Stephan Wilkinson, a good friend and a writer who specializes in cars, planes, and these days about historical battles, too. He is most definitely a curmudgeon, but he's *not* a NASCAR driver! I love Stephan. Brook is Stephan's daughter, and she, too, is a good friend. She lives in San Francisco and writes professionally about eco-tourism and all sorts of related stuff. I love Brook, too.

We've learned much about the Bronx since I wrote this piece, and most of what we've learned came from Dave Wondrich, author of **Imbibe**. Wondrich found reference to the drink on a menu owned by the New-York Historical Society, with the words "about 1895" written in pencil. Since the Zaza cocktail is also on the menu, and since, as Wondrich points out, that cocktail was named for an 1899 play, the menu must be from around 1900. I deciphered the two recipes below from reading between Wondrich's comments in his book (personally I prefer the "à la *Imbibe*" version).

Bronx Cocktail à la *Imbibe*

Recipe derived from David Wondrich's findings in his book, *Imbibe*.

30 ml (1 oz) Plymouth gin

30 ml (1 oz) dry vermouth

30 ml (1 oz) sweet vermouth\

1 teaspoon fresh orange juice

2 dashes orange bitters

Shake over cracked ice and strain into a chilled cocktail glass.

Bronx Cocktail à la Wondrich

Recipe derived from David Wondrich's book, *Imbibe*.

45 ml (1.5 oz) gin (Plymouth, Beefeater, Tanqueray, or "any other good London dry gin")

22.5 ml (.75 oz) fresh orange juice

1 teaspoon dry vermouth

1 teaspoon sweet vermouth

Shake over cracked ice and strain into a chilled cocktail glass.

The Pegu Club Cocktail

The Professor is a little mystified. He just found a crisp, new $50 bill alongside his paycheck, and the Boss doesn't throw bonuses around too easily. He shoots the Boss a question with his eyes.

"Sometimes you're worth your weight in gold, Professor. That's for suggesting we include Cosmopolitans with the brunch package. We've almost doubled Sunday afternoon business in under a month."

"Cosmos? The only thing good about that drink is that it's pink, Professor. What do you have to say about that?" The question comes from Marvin, a retired saloon keeper who's almost as grumpy as the Boss.

"I think it's a typical comment from someone who doesn't know his head from his elbow when it comes to cocktails," The Professor scowls.

Marvin is actually one of The Professor's favorite customers. He's one of those gruff souls with a heart of gold, and he's helped The Professor out more than once with sagely advise on life as well as the business end of the bar trade.

"So prove me wrong, but I suppose I'd better try one before I open my mouth again," says Marvin, throwing another few bills on the bar.

The Professor makes a classic Cosmopolitan while he explains why the drink has merit. The Cosmo follows the same formula as many classic cocktails, the Sidecar and the Margarita among them.

"See, they all start with a base spirit, then add triple sec and either lime or lemon juice. It's a formula that you can apply to just about any spirit and the results are almost guaranteed. One of the secrets, though, is choosing the right triple sec. Most of them are far too sweet for my liking."

"So what do you recommend?"

"Well, I've always used Cointreau in the past, and there's no denying that it's one of the best triple secs on the market, but recently I've found a couple of less expensive brands that rival it —Van Gogh O'Magnifique from Holland and a Mexican orange liqueur called Citronge. I'd recommend either one of these bottlings, or you can spring for the bucks to buy yourself Cointreau."

The common denominator in these three liqueurs is the alcohol content—all are bottled at 40 percent alcohol by volume, whereas the majority of triple secs are far less potent. More alcohol usually makes for a drier, more sophisticated liqueur, and since alcohol has the power to play up any flavors it's mixed with, these triple secs tend to have more prominent orange flavors than lower-proof versions.

"So, let me get this straight—you're telling me that a Cosmo is just a citrus vodka version of the Margarita?" Marvin demands.

"With a little cranberry juice thrown in for color, yes. Good God, Marvin, I do believe I've taught you something."

"Got a gin-based version?"

"A Pegu Club Cocktail is as close as you're gonna get. Wanna try one?"

"Yes, and make one for the Boss, too. Isn't the Pegu Club in Burma?"

"Well, Burma is now known as Myanmar, and Pegu is called Bago, but yes, the drink was named for the club, probably sometime in the twenties. The club was close to the local jail—probably came in handy. It was a pretty raunchy place from what I can gather."

The Professor fixes two Pegu Club Cocktails, serves them to Marvin and the Boss, and breaks his new $50 bill to pay for them himself.

"Nothing I like better than seeing a couple of grouches with nothing to moan about."

"I'll never understand you, Professor."

"That's good, Boss. That's just as it should be."

The Pegu Club Cocktail

60 ml (2 oz) gin
30 ml (1 oz) triple sec
15 ml (.5 oz) fresh lime juice
2 dashes Angostura bitters
1 dash orange bitters, or to taste
Shake over ice and strain into a chilled cocktail glass.

A Word at the End of the Bar

Marvin was based on the now late, very lovable, Marvin Paige, a New York restaurateur who owned a fabulous place called Claire on Seventh Avenue at around 25th Street. I've no idea why I depicted him as grumpy, since he was anything but. Marvin was quiet, and he was a very loving soul. He's greatly missed by many.

All the stuff about the Pegu Club Cocktail holds up today, and although I didn't put this into the column, I thought at the time of writing that the first printed mention of this drink was in *The Savoy Cocktail Book*, 1930, by Harry Craddock. I was wrong. The earliest printed recipe for the Pegu Club Cocktail that's been uncovered thus far (January, 2010) appeared in the 1927 book, *Barflies and Cocktails* by Harry McElhone, famed owner of Harry's New York Bar in Paris. His recipe called for four parts gin, one part orange curaçao, a teaspoon of Rose's lime juice, and a dash each of Angostura and orange bitters. Audrey Saunders, known to many as the Queen of New York's Pegu Club on West Houston, has her own recipe for the cocktail, and I thought it might be good to feature it here for you—she's very exacting with specific brand names and measurements, so if you stick to her formula you'll end up with a perfectly balanced quaff.

Pegu Club Cocktail à la Audrey Saunders

Adapted from a recipe by Audrey Saunders, Pegu Club, New York

60 ml (2 oz) Tanqueray gin

22.5 ml (.75 oz) Marie Brizard orange curaçao

22.5 ml (.75 oz) fresh lime juice

1 dash Angostura bitters

1 dash Pegu Club House Orange Bitters (equal parts Regans' Orange Bitters No. 6 & Fee Brother Orange Bitters)

1 lime wedge, as garnish

Shake over ice and strain the drink into a chilled cocktail glass.

And here's a nice little Kipling quotation for you, just to show how very sophisticated we are:

"In the Pegu Club I found a friend—a Punjabi—upon whose broad bosom I threw myself and demanded food and entertainment." *From Sea to Sea*, Rudyard Kipling, 1889.

Episode 14

The Sazerac

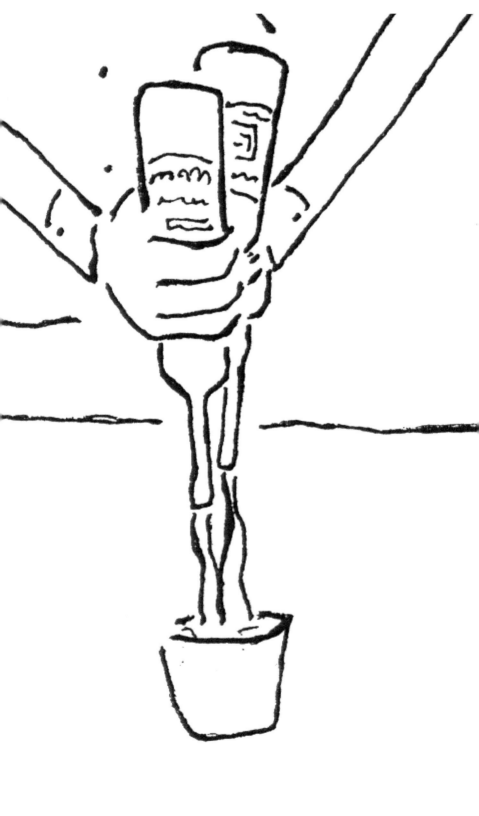

The guy who just walked into The Professor's bar looks vaguely familiar to our favorite cocktailian bartender, but he can't quite place the face. It's Tuesday afternoon, the time when various bartenders congregate at The Professor's bar to swap cocktail recipes and discuss new products, so The Professor leans over the bar and whispers to the assembled mass:

"Any of you know this guy?"

The four bartenders sitting across the mahogany all shake their heads no.

"Do you think you can make me that Sazerac now?" the bearded stranger asks.

This jogs The Professor's memory a little. He had refused to make a Sazerac for someone about a year ago, but he couldn't remember the circumstances.

"You have the advantage, sir," The Professor admits.

"Last time I was in here you were six-deep at the bar, and you told me that you didn't have time to make a true Sazerac. I figured you might not be so busy at this time of the day so I thought I'd give you another chance."

The Sazerac, in its true form, can take a little time to assemble. The methodology involves filling one old-fashioned glass with ice, and in another glass muddling a lemon twist with a sugar cube and bitters before adding ice and the whiskey. The first glass is then emptied, rinsed with an absinthe substitute such as Absente, Herbsaint, or Pernod, and the drink is stirred and strained into it. The Professor used to refuse to make the drink any other way, so when he was too busy, Sazeracs were simply not available.

"Now I remember you. In fact, after that night I revised my methodology, so yes, you can have a Sazerac any old time these days. Bourbon or straight rye whiskey?"

"Come now, aren't you the guy they call The Professor? You can't make a Sazerac with bourbon—far too sweet. What ryes do have back there?"

The Professor is a little miffed. He loves bourbon, and although straight rye whiskey is traditionally the base spirit of choice for this drink, it was originally made with cognac, so he can't see any harm in offering his customers a choice. The rye whiskey made its way into this New Orleans' cocktail in the late 1800s, when the phyloxera epidemic destroyed most of Europe's vines and cognac was hard to come by. The guy with the goatee seems to know what he was talking about, though, so The Professor doesn't push the point.

"I've got Jim Beam, Old Overholt, Sazerac, Rittenhouse Bottled-in-Bond, Van Winkle Family Reserve, Old Potrero, and Wild Turkey. All straight ryes, not that blended whiskey from north of the border that some people call rye."

"Now you're talking, Professor. I'm gonna leave the choice of whiskey in your very capable hands."

The Professor mulls. He's a big fan of Wild Turkey rye. At 101-proof it packs a punch and it's similar in style to the Van Winkle bottling—both are somewhat spicy with some floral notes, and great balance. The Old Potrero isn't quite mature enough for The Professor's taste, and the Sazerac whiskey, at 18 years old, is a bottling he prefers to save for post-prandial sipping, though he's been known to use it in cocktails for the right occasion. The Beam straight rye, like the Old Overholt and the Rittenhouse whiskeys, is very affordable, and any one of them will hold their own very well in a Sazerac, but today The Professor decides to use the Van Winkle bottling.

"Make us one with the Wild Turkey rye while you're at it, Professor, and let's see how you've altered the methodology," yells one of the bartenders.

As The Professor makes the drink he ponders.

"You been reading that new **Esquire Drinks** book by Dave Wondrich? He seems to be a bit of a freak for straight rye, too."

"Yes, I've glanced at it, but not too often since it hit the shelves. Spent far more time reading it when I was writing it," says the stranger.

The Sazerac

15 ml (.5 oz) absinthe substitute (Absente, Herbsaint, or Pernod)
90 ml (3 oz) straight rye whiskey
10 ml (.3 oz) simple syrup
3 dashes Peychaud's bitters
1 lemon twist, as garnish

Pour the absinthe substitute into a chilled champagne flute, swirl the glass to coat the interior, and discard the excess.

Stir the whiskey, syrup, and bitters over ice, and strain into the glass. Add the garnish.

Note: If you can't find Peychaud's bitters in a specialty food store, go to www.sazerac.com for details on how to order.

A Word at the End of the Bar

The world has changed since I wrote this. Now I know Dave Wondrich really well— he's cheap, but he's good on the banter— and now we can get lots more straight ryes, and real absinthe, too. I love the twenty-first century. Here's a revised recipe.

The Sazerac

15 ml (.5 oz) absinthe
60 ml (2 oz) straight rye whiskey
15 ml (.5 oz) simple syrup
3 dashes Peychaud's bitters
1 lemon twist, as garnish

Rinse a chilled old-fashioned glass with the absinthe, add crushed ice and set it aside. Stir the remaining ingredients over ice and set it aside. Discard the ice and any excess absinthe from the prepared glass, and strain the drink into the glass. Add the garnish.

The Uptown Manhattan

The Professor, our cocktailian bartender, is feeling a little under the weather this morning as he opens the bar and allows a couple of regulars to take their usual places at the mahogany.

"What's up, Professor?" asks Doc, a quiet guy who often spends a few hours at the bar with his nose buried in one book or another.

"I can tell you what's wrong with our bartender today. I saw him leaving Harry Denton's Starlight Room in the wee hours of the morning. Not much sleep last night, Professor?" The question comes from Laura, an interior designer who's known to party hard herself on occasion.

The Professor admits to spending a little too much time out on the town last night, but says it was all in the name of research. He had heard that Marcovaldo Dionysos, the Beverage Specialist at Denton's Starlight Room, had come up with a great variation on the Manhattan and decided to investigate the drink for himself.

"Marco put a lot of thought into that drink, and I thought it only fair to sample more than one, so I'd really get the hang of it," The Professor explains.

The Manhattan, usually made with bourbon or straight rye whiskey, sweet vermouth, and a few dashes of bitters, was created in the latter half of the nineteenth century, but nobody is sure who first came up with the drink. A New York City bartender from that period credited "a man named Black, who kept a place ten doors below Houston Street on Broadway," with its invention. The drink is one of the first cocktails to utilize vermouth, but Dionysos substitutes an Itailian *amaro* in its place in his Uptown Manhattan.

"You could say that spirits in the amaro category are spirituous versions of wine-based vermouths—both are flavored with bitter herbs and spices—but amari tend to be an acquired taste. It's said that even Campari, which falls loosely into the amaro category, must be sampled three times before you start to appreciate it," The Professor tells Doc and Laura. "Italians tend to drink them neat, as a *digestivo*, and the flavors are so pronounced that you've gotta be real careful if you use them in cocktails."

Dionysos adds a spoonful of cherry brandy to his Manhattan variation as a counterpoint to the bitter amaro, and he introduces a couple of dashes of orange bitters to the drink, too, making for a very complex potion that's best sipped slowly to appreciate the layers of flavors. And although there are quite a few bottlings he could have chosen— Fratelli Averna, Fernet Branca, Suze, Amer Picon, or Ramazzotti, for instance—he chose Amaro Nonino, a product with softer herbal flavors than most others in this category.

"If you have any memory of last night at all, you can fix me one of those Uptown Manhattans," says Laura. "I was out late, too. Could use something to get the heart started."

The Professor's eyes light up a little. "Not a bad idea, Laura. I'd join you but I've got a whole shift to get through. On the other hand, though, an ounce of amaro might help rid me of this queasy feeling in my stomach."

The Professor fixes Laura's drink and serves it to her in a champagne flute, a glass he far prefers to V-shaped cocktail glasses. For himself, he pours straight amaro into a shot glass. They clink glasses, and while Laura takes her first sip of an Uptown Manhattan, The Professor shoots his drink right back in one gulp.

"Isn't it a little early to be doing shooters, Professor?" The Boss has just walked through the door.

"It's time for dinner in Europe, Boss. Just a little salute to our friends in Italy."

"Boy, you must have had a bad night if you can't come up with anything better than that, Professor. Pour me a shot of

amaro, too. When I finally made it to Denton's last night they told me you'd just left."

The Uptown Manhattan

Adapted from a recipe by Marcovaldo Dionysos, Denton's Starlight Room, San Francisco.

60 ml (2 oz) Maker's Mark bourbon

15 ml (.5 oz) Amaro Nonino

2 dashes orange bitters

1 barspoon cherry brandy from brandied cherries

1 large orange twist, as garnish

1 brandied cherry, as garnish

Shake over ice and strain into a chilled cocktail glass or champagne flute. Hold a lighted match over the glass, take the orange twist in your other hand and hold it by the sides using your thumb and first two fingers. (The colored side of the twist must face the drink.) Hold the twist over the match and squeeze it to release its oils. Add the cherry.

A Word at the End of the Bar

At the time of this writing, Marcovaldo Dionysos holds forth from behind the Clock Bar in San Francisco. He's one of the city's very best cocktailian bartenders and a damned good lad, to boot. I can't stress enough just how fabulous this cocktail is, so if you get a chance, take it for a spin.

Episode 16

The Cable Car

Hal, the regular evening bartender at The Professor's joint, is in Las Vegas for a few days, so The Professor is pulling a night shift for a change. It's just after midnight on Thursday. The bar has been really busy for past few hours, but now things are starting to calm down a little, so The Professor mixes himself a cocktail and starts chatting with the regulars.

"Didn't know Hal was a gambler," says Stuffy, a bartender whose shift has just ended at a nearby gin mill.

"He isn't as far as I know," The Professor tells him. "He went to surprise Tony Abou-Ganim—he's the beverage specialist at the Bellagio Hotel these days. Hal wants to check out the Vegas cocktail scene, so who better than Tony ...?"

"Ah, yes. I miss the lad. Remember his Cable Car Cocktail?"

"Remember it? I've made about a dozen of them to-night. Boy, that drink stuck to this city like glue."

The Cable Car, created by Abou-Ganim in 1996 when he tended bar in San Francisco, calls for Captain Morgan spiced rum, but The Professor also keeps a good selection of other spiced rums behind the bar: Bacardi Spice, Whalers Hawaiian , VooDoo, El Dorado Demerara from Guyana, and Kuya, a new rum from the makers of Kahlúa. Kuya is a "fusion" rum specifically made to marry with cola—the two work well together, especially with a healthy shot of fresh lime juice to balance the sweetness in the soda.

"I got an email from Tony just the other week," says Stuffy. "Seems he just won a gold medal at the Bacardi-Martini & Rossi Bartender's Grand-Prix in Italy."

"Yep, the lad's gone far since he moved to Vegas," says The Professor. "When he first got there, though, he told me he paid nearly twenty bucks for a quart of milk."

"Slot machines in the grocery store?"

"You got it."

The Professor pours Stuffy another three fingers of Irish whiskey and saunters down the bar where a woman is waving a twenty-dollar bill in the air, calling for two Cable Car Cocktails.

As he shakes the drinks the customer asks about Hal, and The Professor goes over to ring the ship's bell on the wall behind the bar.

"What was that all about?" the customer asks.

"You're the hundredth person tonight to ask me that question. He givin' drinks away in here?"

"No. He's just easier on the eyes than his replacement," the customer shoots back, a sly grin on her face.

The Professor scowls for a moment, then returns the grin to let her know she hasn't overstepped her boundaries and gives her the drinks on the house.

"Good to know Hal finally got some loyal regulars," he tells her.

The phone rings, and Regina, the raunchy waitress, dressed tonight in her red leather cowgirl outfit, grabs the receiver and starts to talk. A minute passes, and Regina calls The Professor.

"Think you'd better chat to this guy," she says.

Two minutes later The Professor, shaking his head in disbelief, joins Stuffy again.

"Bad phone call?" asks Stuffy.

"Not real bad. Someone visiting the city for a few of days said he was coming down to surprise Hal. I told him Hal was in Vegas."

"So what's the big deal?"

"The visitor..."

"Oh, no."

"Yep. It's Tony."

The Cable Car

Cinnamon sugar
45 ml (1.5 oz) Captain Morgan spiced rum
22.5 ml (.75 oz) orange curaçao
30 ml (1 oz) fresh lemon juice
15 ml (.5 oz) simple syrup
1 orange twist, as garnish
Moisten the rim of a cocktail glass and coat the exterior with cinnamon sugar (mix granulated sugar and ground cinnamon). Refrigerate to chill. Shake the ingredients over ice and strain into the chilled glass. Add the garnish.

A Word at the End of the Bar

I first met Tony Abou-Ganim when he was behind the stick at Denton's Starlight Lounge in San Francisco. This was after Mardee and I featured two of his drinks in our 1997 book, *New Classic Cocktails*, but his Cable Car came later, and it falls into the same family of drinks as the Margarita and the Sidecar in that it's comprised of a base spirit, an orange-flavored liqueur, and some citrus juice.

I haven't introduced Regina the raunchy waitress thus far in this book, so I guess it's time to let that cat out of the bag. Regina used to work at Painter's, my local joint in the Hudson Valley, and for a few years she was my sidekick when I held my Cocktails in the Country bartender workshops. She's a real person, her name is Regina, and my, oh my, Regina is raunchy. She and I had much fun flirting during those classes, and on one memorable occasion, after we'd exchanged some flirty comments, on of the students stood up, raised his glass, and said, "Here's to you, Mister Robinson." (If you don't understand that, rent *The Graduate*.)

Episode 17

The Tao of Love

The Professor, our cocktailian bartender, is more than a little aggravated with Doogie, a paper conservator from Milwaukee who always visits the bar when he's in town. Doogie is a discerning single malt scotch drinker who doesn't mind paying the price for a good dram, but he hates the thought of good spirits being used in cocktails.

"You mean to tell me that they're charging fifty bucks for one cocktail at the World Bar in Manhattan? Anyone who'd waste half a C-note on a cocktail needs to get his head examined," Doogie rants.

"Their other cocktails aren't that expensive, especially considering it's a pretty swank joint, but this one contains Remy XO cognac and Veuve Cliquot champagne," The Professor explains.

"So why waste the good stuff in a mixed drink? They're idiots, I tell you."

"I'm giving up on you," The Professor tells Doogie, and he wanders up the bar to chat to Broom, a Scottish cocktail freak who better understands that superior ingredients can be the secret to making great mixed drinks.

"They also serve a wonderful drink called the Tao of Love at the World Bar," Broom tells The Professor.

"Yes, their head bartender, George Delgado, came up with it as a Valentine's Day drink, but it caught on fast, so they're serving it year-round now."

"Wanna make one for me?" asks Broom.

"Sure."

The Tao of Love is made with Raynal Tao, a new-ish liqueur with a base of vodka and brandy and a subtle, but very pleasant, citrus flavor. Hpnotiq, another liqueur made with the same base ingredients but flavored with tropical fruits, is a very hot item in liquor stores right now. Aquamarine in color, it's a versatile product that mixes well with just about any spirit, and it changes color depending on what ingredients you mix with it. What makes these two liqueurs stand out most, though, is that neither of them is overly sweet, so both can be used to make very sophisticated cocktails.

The door opens and Linda, Doogie's wife, walks in. Since Broom is closer to the door than Doogie, she stops by to say hi.

"What's that you're drinking, Broom?"

"Have a sip."

Linda loves the Tao of Love, "But I'm in the mood for a Sidecar. Can you make me one with Hennessy Paradis cognac, Professor?"

"Sure thing, Linda," says The Professor, "and how about I top it off with a dash of Veuve Cliquot champagne?"

"Sounds good to me—it was my birthday a few months ago, after all . . ."

As The Professor assembles the drink, he's wearing a sly smirk. Hennessy Paradis is a top-of-the-line bottling that retails for over $250, and the champagne isn't inexpensive, either.

Time passes and Linda walks down the bar to join her husband.

"Guess I owe you for Linda's drink," Doogie says, slapping a crisp, new, hundred-dollar bill on the bar. "Sorry, I don't have anything smaller."

The Professor smiles, ambles to the register, and returns, placing a fifty dollar bill in front of Doogie.

"Sorry, I don't have anything larger," says The Professor.

The Tao of Love

Adapted from a recipe by George Delgado.

3 red raspberries

15 ml (.5 oz) simple syrup

15 ml (.5 oz) fresh lime juice

30 ml (1 oz) Raynal Tao

Chilled champagne

Muddle the raspberries and simple syrup in a mixing glass, then add the lime juice and Raynal Tao. Add ice, shake vigorously. Strain into a champagne flute and top with the champagne.

A Word at the End of the Bar

I've taken lots of stick for saying that Raynal Tao and Hpnotiq are quality products, but I'm going to stick to my guns—I think that they're both well made and valuable to the bartender. Do I drink these liqueurs? No. I drink very few liqueurs on a regular basis. But when I compare these to products to, for instance, Alizé, they stand head and shoulders above it, and there are plenty of punters out there who like sweet drinks.

It's the job of the bartender to keep everyone hap-py—not just people with what are considered to be sophisticated tastes. Liking sweet drinks don't make 'em bad people, you know.

I do have a friend in Milwaukee who is a paper con-servator. His name is Doug Stone, his wife is Linda, and we've been friends since the mid-nineties when he con-tacted me with some question or other about whisky, I think. Broom wasn't well know when this column first appeared, but Dave Broom is now internationally fa-mous in the world of fine spirits, and he is a mutual friend of Doug, Linda, and myself. He's a Scot with lots of whisky wisdom and holds forth regularly on the sub-ject in *Whisky* magazine.

Episode 18

The Chas Cocktail

I t's three o'clock in the afternoon, the bar is empty, and The Professor, our cocktailian bartender, is polishing the bottles on the backbar. The door opens and a guy glides down the bar on a Segway HT transporter— the motor-powered vehicle that looks like an old-fashioned lawn mower with wheels on the sides and a place to stand where the blade would be. He parks his Segway next to the coatrack and takes a bar stool close to the jukebox. The Professor, deciding to ignore the weird contraption, stops what he's doing and ambles over to his new customer.

"You must like that seat," says The Professor.
"What makes you say that?"
"That's where you sat last time you were here."

"Jeez, that was over a year ago. I know only one other bartender who can do that—Murray Stenson. Zig Zag Café, Seattle."

The Professor has heard about Stenson, a guy who has tended bar for more than a couple of decades in the Emerald City. Known to some of his regular customers as "The Blur" because he moves so quickly when business is brisk, Stenson also has a reputation for remembering how everyone likes their drinks and for making sure that the whole bar is happy. He's the kind of bartender that The Professor strives to be.

"Can't remember what you were drinking, though. Guess I've lost a few too many brain cells."

"I can't remember what I was drinking then, either, but perhaps you'd like to fix me a Chas Cocktail—it's one of Murray's creations," says the customer, who goes on to tell The Professor how to make the drink.

Stenson created the Chas Cocktail out of frustration one night, for one of his regular customers who loves bourbon but refuses to drink the same cocktail twice during the course of an evening. It's an unusual potion since it calls for whiskey and four different liqueurs: amaretto, Bénédictine, Cointreau, and orange curaçao. The Cointreau and curaçao are both orange-flavored, but curaçao tends to be far sweeter than the dry triple sec found in the Cointreau bottle. Amaretto, flavored mainly with peach pits that impart an almond flavor, is another sweet liqueur—Disaronno is the most popular bottling in this category—and Bénédictine has a strong honey flavor with a complex backdrop of herbs and spices. Bénédictine tends to be one of those liqueurs that people must try twice before they appreciate it, but it can add wonderful nuances to a cocktail when used sparingly.

The Professor makes two Chas Cocktails, one for his customer and one for himself. They clink glasses and take a sip.

"I was worried that this would be too sweet, and it *is* sweet, but it's a really well-balanced drink," says The Professor. "I've got to get up there one of these days and meet Murray Stenson."

"If you ever get to Zig Zag, tell 'em Phil sent you. That should get you thrown out in a hurry."

"You ride that thing into Zig Zag?" The Professor asks, pointing at the Segway.

"Tried to once, but had a little accident, I'm afraid. It was my third bar of the night."

"Too many drinks to keep your balance?"

"Balance isn't an issue on one of those things—I just wasn't thinking about the stairway that leads to the joint."

The Chas Cocktail

Adapted from a recipe by Murray Stenson, Zig-Zag, Seattle.

37.5 ml (1.25 oz) bourbon

3.75 ml (.125 oz) amaretto

3.75 ml (.125 oz) Cointreau

3.75 ml (.125 oz) Bénédictine

3.75 ml (.125 oz) orange curaçao

1 orange twist, as garnish

Stir all of the ingredients over ice and strain into a chilled cocktail glass. Add the garnish.

A Word at the End of the Bar

Murray Stenson is a legend, and deservedly so. He's perhaps the quintessential bartender since he not only creates fabulous drinks and is known for his speed and accuracy behind the bar, but he's also a very generous soul who really cares about his customers. I was privileged to stand behind the bar with Murray at Zig Zag in 2009. Another ambition realized.

Episode 19

The Velvet Fog

The Professor, our cocktailian bartender, is a very happy man today. He just signed off on a liquor delivery and three bottles of a new product called Velvet Falernum were in one of the cases. Falernum is a low-alcohol liqueur made with sugarcane and flavored with limes and other ingredients such as almonds and cloves. The Boss walks through the door to find The Professor tasting a little falernum from a shot glass.

"Professor, we aren't even open yet and you're doing shooters. What the heck are you playing at?" he explodes.

"And good morning to you, too, Boss. It's rare to see you in such fine fettle at this hour," The Professor replies.

"Yeah, well, I'm having a problem with that waitress Regina. I threatened to institute a dress code if she keeps wearing those outfits—she showed up last night looking like a showgirl from Cabaret." The Boss wanders downstairs to his office, mumbling and grumbling as he goes, and The Professor turns to greet Jen, a bartender from a nearby joint.

"Did the falernum get here?" she asks.

"Sure did. Want a shot?"

Jen takes a sip and the two cocktailians start to discuss how they are going to use it in mixed drinks. The Professor thinks it would work well as an additional ingredient in a Manhattan, and Jen wants to try mixing it with peaty single malts such as Ardbeg, Laphroaig, or Lagavulin.

"Dale DeGroff sent me this recipe for a drink he calls Velvet Fog," says Jen, pulling her notepad from her bag. "Want to try it?"

"Sure. I hear that he's been doing a great job training bartenders in London, but I sometimes wish he was still behind the stick at New York's Rainbow Room," says The Professor.

The cocktailian duo are in awe of the Velvet Fog. Not only does it have a wonderfully complex palate, the freshly grated nutmeg floating on the cocktail makes it an aromatic masterpiece, too. The door opens and Regina strides up to the bar, wearing a pill-box hat and looking something like an airline stewardess from the movie *Catch Me if You Can*. She asks if the Boss is in the office

and disappears downstairs. Jen is just finishing her cocktail when Regina reappears from the office.

"You still work here?" asks The Professor.

"Sure do. Probably for as long as I like. Did I tell you that my dad used to hang out at the bar where the Boss worked back in the seventies?"

"Don't tell me you have something on the Boss, Regina?"

"Not really. Just this picture of him tending bar."

Regina hands a photograph to The Professor who takes a glance, smiles, and gives it back.

"Is the Boss wearing some hideous hippie clothes in that picture?" asks Jen.

"No," smiles Regina. "He isn't wearing a stitch."

The Velvet Fog

Adapted from a recipe by Dale DeGroff.

45 ml (1.5 oz) Stolichnaya Ohranj vodka

15 ml (.5 oz) fresh lime juice

30 ml (1 oz) Velvet Falernum

30 ml (1 oz) fresh orange juice

1 dash Angostura bitters

1 orange twist, as garnish

Freshly grated nutmeg, as garnish

Shake the ingredients over ice and strain into a chilled cock-tail glass. Hold a lighted match over the glass, take the orange twist in your other hand and hold it by the sides using your thumb and first two fingers. (The colored side of the twist must face the drink.) Hold the twist over the match and squeeze it to release its oils. The oils will ignite as they leap through the flame, caramelizing before they rest on the top of the drink. Add the nutmeg.

A Word at the End of the Bar

Velvet Falernum had just made its USA comeback when this column first appeared, I think, and it's been very well received. It's imported by the wonderful Eric Seed, and here's what his web site, alpenz.com, has to say about it: "Velvet Falernum is a longtime staple item of resorts and bars in Barbados, and today for its use in tropical, tiki and Caribbean drinks such as the Rum Swizzle, Mai Tai, Zombie, Royal Bermuda Yacht Club and the Corn n' Oil. It is made from an infusion of spices and lime juice in sugarcane syrup and Barbados Rum. John D. Taylor's Falernum is considered by many as the original Falernum, and is today produced by famed rum distiller R.L. Seale, Ltd." Almonds, ginger, and cloves are commonly used to flavor falernum.

Having the Boss tending bar naked in the 1970s in this piece was a nod to Norman Smith, who tended bar at The Mad Hatter and Bayard's back then, and the late David Ridings, one of my oldest and dearest friends.

Dave tended bar at Drake's Drum before opening his own joint, Ridings, and later Paddington's in the seventies and early eighties. All these bars were on Manhattan's Upper East Side. One night in the early seventies, on a bet, Ridings and Smith tended bar for one hour, stark naked, at Drake's Drum, and Norman is famous for telling everyone that he couldn't get a date for months after that went down. I didn't witness this event—it happened before my 1973 arrival in New York.

The Fish House Cocktail

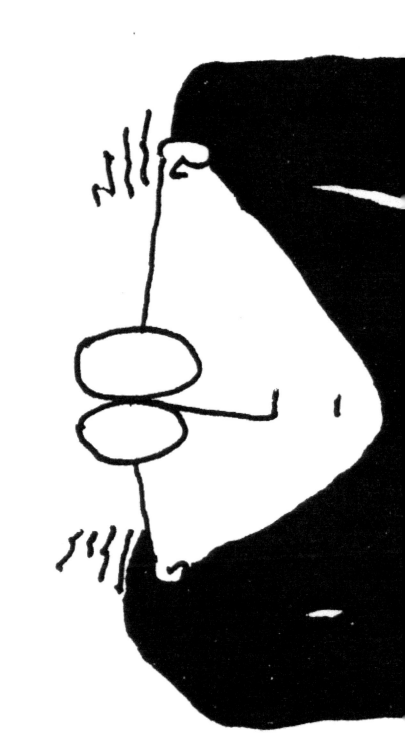

Doc, a regular customer at The Professor's bar, has been poring over an old book for most of the afternoon, sipping coffee after coffee, along with a couple of single malts. He finally closes the book and asks for a glass of Fish House Punch.

"What are you reading now? Seems to me you never order mixed drinks unless they're mentioned in some book or other," says The Professor.

"*The Saga of American Society*. Dixon Wector. Not a bad read at all, and yes, he mentions Fish House Punch. Gonna make some for me?"

"Nope. I'm not making a whole bowl of punch so you can have one glass before you go home. Let's look at the recipe, though. Perhaps we can turn it into a cocktail."

Fish House Punch was created at the State in Schuylkill, a Pennsylvania fishing club founded in 1732. According to Wector, "under its first governor, Thomas Stretch, it was organized like a miniature commonwealth . . . with executive, legislative, and judicial branches represented among its thirty members, who were called 'citizens.'" The recipe for the punch was a closely guarded secret until it was inadvertently released at a debutante's ball, circa 1900.

The Professor takes a notebook out of a drawer behind the bar and finds his hand-written recipe for the punch.

"Sheesh! Rum, brandy, peach brandy, lemon juice, lime juice, and sugar. It's unusual to see two spirits in one drink, but when it happens, rum and brandy are usually the ones you see together. The peach brandy poses a little problem here, too. The peach brandy we use today is usually a sweet liqueur, but chances are when this punch was first made, it was more like a calvados made from peaches instead of apples. Probably not aged for too long, either—purposefully aging spirits wasn't common until the end of the 1700s."

"I'd better have a scotch while you think about this. Let me try that new Glenlivet 2003 Cellar Collection bottling."

"It'll set you back twenty bucks. Vintage 1983, it's finished in French oak."

"Finished?"

"Yeah, finished. They transfer it to new barrels for the last two or three years of aging. Darned good dram, though—a little fruitier than you might expect from Glenlivet, but it has its dry side, too."

The Professor serves Doc a generous tot of whisky and starts to scribble in his notebook. Doc's glass is almost drained by the time The Professor comes up with a formula for a cocktail based on the punch. He makes the drink, straining it into a chilled champagne flute for Doc and saving a little for himself to sample.

"This is great, Professor," says Doc, after taking a couple of sips.

"Thanks, Doc. Yeah, it's a decent drink. You've got to be careful with this, though. George Washington drank Fish House Punch when he visited the State in Schuylkill."

"And what happened?"

"Nobody knows. He didn't make an entry in his diary for the next three days . . . "

The Fish House Cocktail

45 ml (1.5 oz) dark rum
15 ml (.5 oz) brandy
15 ml (.5 oz) peach brandy
15 ml (.5 oz) simple syrup
7.5 ml (.25 oz) fresh lime juice
7.5 ml (.25 oz)s fresh lemon juice
Shake over ice and strain into a chilled champagne flute.

A Word at the End of the Bar

The story about Washington not making diary entries after his visit to the Fish House Club is, as far as I can make out, not much more than a rumor, but in his book, *Imbibe*, David Wondrich attests that Washington did visit the State in Schuylkill in 1787, and we never argue with Wondrich.

I steal from Wondrich on a regular basis, and when it comes to deciphering his recipes, he doesn't make it easy on me. Nonetheless, I labored through his fabulous prose on this drink to come up with a workable recipe for you, so the one below is an updated version of the one that appeared in the *Chronicle*, and it's probably far closer to the original.

The Fish House Cocktail Revised, 2010

60 ml (2 oz) brandy
30 ml (1 oz) aged rum
5 ml (1 tsp) peach brandy
15 ml (.5 oz) simple syrup (made with Demerara sugar)
15 ml (.5 oz) fresh lemon juice
Shake over ice and strain into a chilled cocktail glass.

Episode 21

The Double Shot

The Boss is very pleased with himself today—he just won a couple of grand on the lottery. "Don't tell a soul," he orders The Professor, our cocktailian bartender, "Everyone will expect me to buy drinks." The Professor nods as the Boss leaves the bar, and within half an hour there are half a dozen bartenders from local restaurants sitting across the mahogany—they are there for their weekly discussion about drinks, new and old, and to tell each other about new products they've sampled recently.

"I've tasted a new rum, a new liqueur, and a new cocktail that calls for both of them," says Robert, a guy who works in a chic cocktail lounge just a couple of blocks way from The Professor's joint. "And the recipe comes from a chef, not a bartender. Seems to know his stuff, too."

"Yep. Good chefs are naturals when it comes to cocktails. Who's the chef in question?" asks The Professor.

"Bruce Tanner. He's done quite a bit of work with distilled spirits, and he sometimes works at the James Beard Foundation. Want to taste the ingredients for this drink? I brought them along."

The group takes sips of Santa Teresa 1796 rum from Venezuela, and Rhum Orange liqueur, a product made by the same company. Everyone is impressed with the quality of both products—the rum is quite dry, with some peppery notes under rich vanilla flavors, and the liqueur packs a powerful punch of orange zest with a hint of spices such as cardamom. It's the liqueur that provokes discussion, though.

"I understand how these two ingredients would work well together," says The Professor, "but I hope he's gone easy on the liqueur—it's fairly sweet. Lets try some other orange liqueurs, too."

The Professor starts to pour samples from a variety of orange-flavored liqueurs, and the assembled bevy of bartenders tastes each one in turn. Domanier Cognac à L'Orange Grand Liqueur is even sweeter than the Rhum Orange, and it's pretty one dimensional, but Extase XO Liqueur d'Orange & Cognac XO offers a great spiciness and a dry finish to boot. They try Gran Gala liqueur from Italy and find it to be well balanced, with both sweet and spicy notes in the finish, and then they sample three different bottlings of Grand Marnier, all three made with a cognac base.

The regular bottling is bold and lush, with a peppery finish the gang adores, and although they enjoy the nutty characteristics of the 150th anniversary bottling, it's the 100th anniversary Grand Marnier that everyone agrees is the best. The body is thick, syrupy, and buttery, and the palate shows a wonderfully bitter orange zest with notes of almonds and dates. All this, and the finish is very dry, making it ideal as a cocktail ingredient.

"Okay, now let's look at the recipe for this drink. What else goes in there?" asks The Professor.

"Lime juice and Angostura bitters," Robert tells him. "Initially I didn't think there was enough lime juice to balance the liqueur, but the bitters come to the rescue in this drink."

"Yes, I've seen that happen quite often. When a drink is palatable but something seems to be missing, Angostura can often make a huge difference. I wouldn't go for Peychaud's bitters in this case—they're sweeter than Angostura—and orange bitters would just be overkill on the orange theme. Hand the recipe over and I'll make it up."

Robert hands the recipe for the Double Shot to The Professor, who starts to prepare the drink as the other bartenders watch. The door opens and the Boss quietly walks back into the bar. Thinking that nobody noticed his entrance, he stands in the corner, watching The Professor. Robert, however, saw the Boss out of the corner of his eye and decides to have some fun.

"Come on, Professor. Won't you let us pay for just one drink today?" he says, with a wink.

The Professor catches on quickly. "Not today, Robert. The Boss said something about drinks on the house before he left."

The Double Shot

Adapted from a recipe by Bruce Tanner, James Beard Foundation.

60 ml (2 oz) Santa Teresa 1796 rum

45 ml (1.5 oz) Rhum Orange liqueur

10 ml (.3 oz) fresh lime juice

1 dash Angostura bitters

Shake the ingredients over ice and strain into a chilled cocktail glass.

A Word at the End of the Bar

I n the early 1970s, when I tended bar at Drake's Drum on New York's Upper East Side, an Australian guy by the name of Randall George was one of my customers. Randall was also a bartender, though I can't remember where he strutted his stuff, and he was a great guy but a bit of a prankster. It was he who would ask me, "Can't I pay for just one drink in this place?" whenever Jim Duke, my boss, was within earshot. Cheers, Randall.

Episode 22

The Pumpkin Martini

The Professor, our cocktailian bartender, is yet again working a night shift, something he usually abhors. But this is a special occasion—the Boss, always eager to make a few extra bucks, is holding an early Halloween party on what is typically a slow night at the bar, and the joint is jumpin'.

The Professor is dressed as Alex from *A Clockwork Orange*, complete with false eyelashes on one eye and a bowler hat; the Boss, appropriately, is wearing a 1920s gangster-style suit and sporting a very realistic fake scar on his face; and Regina, the raunchy waitress, has mysteriously donned a very conservative business suit—grey pin-stripes with a skirt that reaches past her knees, and a white silk blouse buttoned to the neck.

"Who are you supposed to be?" asks The Professor

"You don't know?"

"Not a clue."

"Good." She leaves him hanging and takes a tray of gorgeous orange-colored drinks to a table full of revelers dressed as flappers with rouged knees, and stockings rolled down to their ankles.

"What the heck are those drinks?" the Boss asks The Professor.

"Pumpkin Martinis. Got the recipe from Maggiano's in San Jose. Selling like wild fire tonight."

"What's in them, Professor?"

"I'm kinda busy trying to get money into your register right now, Boss," The Professor grouches as he walks down the bar to take an order from a guy dressed as the Phantom of the Opera who's having problems keeping his mask on his face and drinking at the same time.

Maggiano's is part of a nationwide chain of Italian restaurants, and the Pumpkin Martini was created by David Pennachetti, Director of Beverages. The drink is a simple affair that calls for pumpkin liqueur, spiced rum, and half and half, but it's a great cocktail for late autumn.

There are so many flavors of liqueurs on the market in the twenty-first century that it's possible to make drinks that taste of almost any fruit, nut, and herb under the sun, but one of

the keys to selecting a good liqueur is to look for the percentage of alcohol in the bottle. You'll pay more for a higher alcohol content, but the alcohol actually boosts the flavors in the liqueur, and adds a sophisticated dryness to the product. Bols and Marie Brizard are very good brands- with extensive ranges of flavors, and both the Mathilde and Edmond Briottet lines, while not hugely wide-ranging, are superb products.

Suddenly Regina climbs onto a bar stool and from there onto the bar, where she stands in front of the crowd and starts to rip off her clothes. They are held together with Velcro, so it doesn't take long before her suit and blouse are lying on the floor. The Boss has turned his head and is cringing at the end of the bar.

"Tell me she's not naked," he pleads with The Professor.

"Who? You mean Supergirl?" The Professor snickers. And with that Regina, now in her caped super-heroine costume, leaps off the bar right onto the Boss's back.

"Just trying to make the city streets safer for the citizens," she says. "Al Capone, you've been a very naughty boy."

The Pumpkin Martini

Adapted from a recipe by created by David Pennachetti, Director of Beverages, Maggiano's Little Italy Restaurant.

90 ml (3 oz) Bols Pumpkin Smash liqueur

30 ml (1 oz) Captain Morgan Original Spiced Rum

1 dash half and half

Cinnamon sugar

Ground cinnamon, as garnish

Shake the ingredients over ice, and strain into a cocktail glass rimmed with cinnamon sugar. Sprinkle a little ground cinnamon on top.

A Word at the End of the Bar

This story takes me back to a bar called Ridings, where I worked from 1977 until 1979, if memory serves. It was owned by Bob Young, a guy who worked for IBM, and Dave Ridings, an old friend of mine from the UK who, sadly, went up to hold forth from behind the stick in that barroom in the sky back in 2000.

We had fabulous adventures at Ridings—it was a very solid neighborhood bar where "everybody knew your name," and everybody cared for each other, too. One of the customers, though I can't remember who it was, threw a come-as-your-favorite-fantasy party one Halloween, and that party was the basis for this story. I went as Alex from *A Clockwork Orange*, and Mary Ball, a friend and customer who lived in the apartment above the bar, did the Supergirl thing. She didn't rip her clothes off in from of everyone, though, she just went to the bathroom in her business suit, and came out as Supergirl. That was one helluva party.

Episode 23

The Blood and Sand Cocktail

A suave, sophisticated gentleman is sitting at The Professor's bar, quietly sipping a Dry Gin Martini. Two stools down from him, Doc, one of The Professor's regulars, has his nose buried in **Blood and Sand**, a novel by Vincente Blasco Ibáñez about the rise and fall of a bullfighter. The book was made into a movie starring Rudolf Valentino in the 1920s.

"Would you like to drink that book?" The Professor asks Doc.

"Huh?"

"Blood and Sand. It's a cocktail, you know."

The Professor goes on to tell Doc about this unique drink, and he can't help but notice that the stranger is eavesdropping on the conversation. The Blood and Sand Cocktail, which dates back to at least 1930, calls for scotch, sweet vermouth, cherry brandy, and orange juice, and traditionally equal amounts of all four ingredients are used. The Professor often makes the drink into a highball by adding extra orange juice, and many of his regulars drink it that way alongside brunch.

Although this drink can be made with a just about any scotch, each one adding its own nuance to the cocktail, it's important to use the correct style of cherry brandy to achieve the proper balance. Some cherry brandies are eaux de vie, and they are often called kirschwasser, especially if they're made in Europe. Eaux de vie are typically not aged; they are very dry in character, and clear, like vodka, in color. This style of cherry brandy should be sipped neat, often well-chilled in the freezer, after dinner.

The style of cherry brandy to use in the Blood and Sand Cocktail is a sweet liqueur, usually deep red in color, and usually bearing almond flavors as well as cherry. The two most highly regarded brand names of this type are Cherry Heering, a Danish product made from sour cherries and aged in oak for around three years, and Cherry Marnier, a French product made with Dalmatian cherries. Both of these bottlings are drier, more complex, and far more sophisticated than most of the other cherry brandies on the market.

"So how is that book?" The Professor asks Doc.

"Not bad at all—I'm renting the movie tonight. Did you know there was a famous bullfighter from San Francisco? Barnaby Conran was his name."

"Conrad," the stranger corrects him.

"Think you're wrong, my friend. It was Conran. He used to run a nightclub here called El Toreador."

"El Matador, actually."

"What, the joint where Agnes Moorhead danced a Flamenco on the bar?"

"I think you'll find that that was Ava Gardner."

Doc, in a curmudgeonly mood, shakes his head, rolls his eyes, and goes back to reading his book. The stranger orders a second Martini.

"Two parts gin to one part vermouth and a dash of orange bitters again?" asks The Professor.

"Yes, please. I like my Martinis the old-fashioned way."

"There's a book called **The Martini** that gives that exact recipe," says The Professor. "Can't for the life of me think of the author, though."

Doc looks up from his book with a puzzled look on his face. "Wait a minute—that was Conran's son, Barnaby Conran III," he says. "It's all coming back to me now."

"I'm quite sure his name is Conrad," says the stranger.
"He wrote a total of 27 books. He was also vice consul to Spain,
an art teacher, at one point he was a secretary to the novelist
Sinclair Lewis."

"Sounds as though you know your stuff. Perhaps he is
called Conrad, after all," Doc concedes.

"Yes, I think you'll find I'm correct. There's very little I don't know about my father."

The Blood and Sand Cocktail

22.5 ml (.75 oz) scotch
22.5 ml (.75 oz) sweet vermouth
22.5 ml (.75 oz) cherry brandy
22.5 ml (.75 oz) fresh orange juice
Shake over ice and strain into a chilled cocktail glass.

A Word at the End of the Bar

This was just a tip of the hat to Barnaby Conrad III, a charming gent, indeed. The drink's a doozy. Dale DeGroff introduced me to this one when he was still working the Rainbow Room in New York. I feel so bloody lucky to have known him back then.

Episode 24

The James Joyce Cocktail

The Professor, our cocktailian bartender, has just returned from a trip to Ireland, the country of his ancestors, and he can't stop talking about his vacation to his regular customers. He's been bending the ear of Doc, a guy who spends many afternoons reading all sorts of books, for over half an hour now, and Doc has been patiently listening.

"Then, on Saturday night, I went on what they call a literary pub crawl in Dublin," says The Professor. "A couple of actors take a group of people around pubs where famous Irish writers used to hang out. You have a drink in each pub, and the actors read from various works or act out scenes from plays and the like. It was wonderful. You end up with a belly full of Guinness, and you can say it was a learning experience, too."

"Sounds like that's right up my street. If I ever get to Dublin I'll do that," says Doc, enthusiastically.

It's just after five o'clock and the bar is getting busy now, so The Professor has to deal with the crowd. Still, he can't get his mind off his vacation, and he's suggesting various brands of Irish whiskey to anyone who'll listen.

Although most Irish whiskey is blended, there are some single malt bottlings on the market. Knappogue Castle, for instance, is a single malt Irish whiskey that is issued in various vintages—the oldest one was made in 1951, but this bottling might have spent a little too long in the wood. The 1990, 1991, and 1992 vintages, though, are wonderful whiskeys with complex palates, and smooth, sweet bodies. These are connoisseur bottlings that are well worth seeking out.

The Bushmills Distillery, in Northern Ireland, offers three single malt Irish whiskeys: a 10-year-old that's extremely smooth and malty in the mouth, but has a clean, dry finish; and a 16-year-old that's aged first in bourbon casks, and then spends time maturing in oloroso sherry butts and port pipes—this one is extremely complex, and hints of port can be found in the palate. The third single malt from Bushmills is a 21-year-old that's aged in a combination of bourbon barrels and sherry butts. This is an incredibly good dram with hints of raisins and caramel, and even a touch of bittersweet chocolate peeks through.

The crowd at The Professor's bar is getting deeper by the minute, and although our bartender has everything under control, he's having to move very quickly to keep everyone happy. He's straining what was supposed to have been an Oriental Cocktail—a drink from **The Savoy Cocktail Book**, 1930—into a chilled champagne flute for Doc, and Doc is giving him a strange look.

"What's wrong?" asks The Professor.

"You just made my drink with Irish whiskey instead of straight rye." He takes a sip, and says, "It's darned good, though. And remember, mistakes are the portals of discovery."

"What?"

"It's a quote from James Joyce—didn't you learn anything on that literary pub crawl?"

"I had no pen, no ink, no table, no room, no time, no quiet, no inclination," The Professor quotes Joyce back to Doc. "And the drink you're sipping is now officially called the James Joyce Cocktail," he declares.

The James Joyce Cocktail

A variation on the Oriental Cocktail, created by Gary Regan, 2003.

45 ml (1.5 oz) Irish whiskey

22.5 ml (.75 oz) sweet vermouth

22.5 ml (.75 oz) triple sec

15 ml (.5 oz) fresh lime juice

Shake all the ingredients over ice and strain into a chilled cocktail glass.

A Word at the End of the Bar

This one brings back memories of a very drunken press trip to Ireland, and the literary pub crawl was one of the fabulous events on said trip. Surprisingly, I remember it quite well. I've had some pretty fabulous times in Ireland, both in the North and in the Republic, and whenever I think of the Republic, my mind wanders to the beautiful town of Kinsale, and a few hours on a fishing boat there back in 1999. I wrote about it in the Ardent Spirits newsletter. Here's how that tale went:

The Man Who Caught a Fish

I was recently invited to join a bunch of rowdy journalists on a trip to Ireland to visit, among other things, the Old Jameson Distillery in Dublin and the Midleton Distillery in County Cork. It was a swell visit, even though I spent most of my time trying to keep the other writers under control. Terry Sullivan, bon-vivant extraordinaire and author of the Mixology column in **GQ** magazine, was even more gregarious than the rest of the crew and I found myself having to stay up late each and every night just to make sure he didn't get into trouble.

Luckily I had help in the form of the ever smiling Eily Kilgannon from Irish Distillers, and she also managed to keep an eye on Terry when she wasn't too busy buying round after round of Jameson's wonderful Irish whiskey.

Toward the end of the trip we were treated to a fishing trip in County Cork, and after I managed to drag the rest of the crowd from the bar and herd them on board the boat, Eily plied everyone with a miniature or two of Jameson's to keep them from complaining. I, of course, declined at first, but when I noticed a tear starting to well in Eily's eyes, I succumbed to temptation.

The waves were rolling that day, and it was somewhat difficult for me to find time to actually fish since I was so busy tending to the people on board who, well, weren't feeling their best. But I persevered, throwing my line into the sea again and again, until I was finally rewarded with a huge mackerel, big enough to share with everyone else when the boat finally docked. Okay—it was about 6 inches long and the captain kept it.

I don't think that any other distinguished members of the press actually caught a fish that day. In fact, I've been told by more than a few people that I was, indeed, the only man to catch a fish. However, I'm not the sort to boast, so let's just keep it to ourselves. But if you should ever bump into Terry (his column is wonderful), you'd do me a favor if you just asked him politely whether or not he caught anything that day. I doubt it, but you never know.

Winner of the First Annual Ardent Spirits-Jameson's Irish Whiskey Limerick Competition

During the trip to Ireland we organized a competition among the travelers to see who could come up with the best Limerick containing the word "Jameson" by the end of the week. The winner was the above mentioned Terry Sullivan, who was awarded yet more Jameson's whiskey. His little eyes lit up. Here's Terry's winning entry which, strangely enough, mentions yours truly:

"Gary Regan could hardly refuse
An offer of yet more free booze
He cracked open the Jameson
As he put his pajamas on
Said 'I'll drink to my own health, that's whose.'"

Episode 25

The Bottled Sidecar DeLuxe
&The Bottled Jack Rose Royale

"**P**rofessor, could we please throw just a couple of dozen of these empty liquor bottles away?" the Boss is pleading with our cocktailian bartender.

Jen, a local bartender who's always trying to hone her craft, asks The Professor what he's going to do with the bottles— it's the first time she's spent December in San Francisco, so she's not yet acquainted with The Professor's holiday ritual.

"I'll be making bottled cocktails to take to parties—I usually get invited to one or two soirees around this time of year," The Professor tells her. "You know how to make bottled cocktails?"

"No, is there a trick to it?"

There's no real trick to making cocktails in bottles, but it's imperative to think about the particular ingredients that make up a regular cocktail: There's probably a base spirit, such as rum or brandy, perhaps there's a liqueur to sweeten the drink, and something akin to lemon juice might be added to balance the sweetness of the liqueur. And then there's the water that melts from the ice when the drink is mixed. That water is the secret ingredient in bottled cocktails.

The best thing about making bottled cocktails for parties is that, if you omit the water initially, you can make these drinks days in advance—most cocktail recipes call for enough distilled spirits to keep the mixture stable for a long time. The water must be added at least six hours before serving, and the bottles must be refrigerated for at least that long so they can be poured straight from the bottle.

To calculate how much water you need in any cocktail that you intend to bottle, simply take the sum of all the other ingredients, and divide by three—this will make sure that the drink is well-balanced. And try to use bottled water that doesn't have a great deal of flavor—Poland Spring is The Professor's choice in this regard.

"So which cocktails are you making this year?" Jen asks The Professor.

"I know I have a good stock of Laird's Applejack and Chambord, the French liqueur made from black raspberries, so I'm thinking of making a variation on the Jack Rose, using the Chambord instead of grenadine."

"You have Grand Marnier at home, too? You could make a cool Sidecar using that instead of the triple sec." suggests Jen.

"You psychic or something?" The Boss slams a bottle of the 100-year anniversary bottling of Grand Marnier onto the bar—it's The Professor's favorite bottling of this liqueur. "A present from the ex-wife—it would have been our anniversary today. Think it's supposed to remind me we didn't last as long as a bottle of French cordial. Take it home. Please." He leaves the bar in his usual huff.

"How long were they married?" asks Jen.

"Ever hear the word 'fortnight'?"

The Bottled Sidecar DeLuxe

Makes 660 ml (22 oz)

360 ml (12 oz) cognac

90 ml (3 oz) Grand Marnier

90 ml (3 oz) fresh lemon juice

180 ml (6 oz) bottled water

Lemon twists, as garnishes

If preparing more than six hours ahead of time, combine the cognac, Grand Marnier, and lemon juice in a bottle. Shake well, and set aside. Six hours ahead of usage, add the water, shake well, cover, and refrigerate. To serve, pour into chilled cocktail glasses, and add a lemon twist to each drink.

The Bottled Jack Rose Royale

Makes 660 ml (22 oz)

360 ml (12 oz) Laird's Applejack

75 ml (2.5 oz) Chambord black raspberry liqueur

75 ml (2.5 oz) fresh lemon juice

150 ml (5 oz) bottled water

Maraschino cherries, as garnishes

If preparing more than six hours ahead of time, combine the applejack, Chambord, and lemon juice in a bottle. Shake well, and set aside. Six hours ahead of usage, add the water, shake well, cover, and refrigerate. To serve, pour into chilled cocktail glasses, and add a maraschino cherry to each drink.

A Word at the End of the Bar

I must say that taking bottled cocktails to dinner parties makes it awfully easy to be a very welcome guest, and I do this quite frequently. Regular citizens love having someone shake up fresh cocktails for them, so sometimes I'll make up the cocktails without water, and I'll take a shaker, barspoon, and strainer to the party with me, too. If you do this, it's best to pick up a bag or two of ice on your way to the party—few people keep enough ice on hand for this kind of thing.

Woolf Barnato & The Bentley Cocktail

The Professor is aving a wonderful afternoon with David, a vintage car freak who likes to pass time with our cocktailian bartender whenever he's in town.

"I'm telling you, Bentleys are 'in,' Professor. It's the car to be seen in—a Bentley won the Le Mans again this year, you know."

"First time since 1927?" The Professor asks.

David is confused—The Professor knows nothing about cars or racing, but he's pretty close to the mark with his 1927 date.

"No, it's the first time since 1930, but '27 was the first year a Bentley won the race. How the heck do you know that?"

"It's the stuff of cocktailian legend, my friend," says The Professor, planting his elbows on the bar, bringing his face close to David's, and in hushed tones, relating the tale: "The Bentley Cocktail is detailed in the 1930 edition of *The Savoy Cocktail Book* by Harry Craddock, and we know that the Bentley Boys celebrated their 1927 Le Mans victory at the London Savoy. They even managed to get the car itself into the dining room—carried the darned thing up the staircase. The question is, though, did Craddock create the drink? He doesn't claim it as his own in the book. Just leaves us hanging. Nobody really knows the truth. It drives people crazy."

The Bentley Cocktail is a simple affair—it's made of equal parts of Dubonnet Rouge and Calvados or apple brandy, but it packs quite a punch, and it's a sophisticated mélange of flavors—not sweet at all. David has another Bentley-related drink up his sleeve, though . . .

"Perhaps you could make me a Woolf Barnato cocktail, Professor?"

"Oh, Salim Khoury's new drink? The one named for the guy who won Le Mans three years in a row while he was chairman of Bentley about 70 years ago?"

"Thought I might stump you with that one," David unhappily confesses.

"Nah, the whole cocktailian community's keeping an eye on Khoury. Being the new head honcho at the Savoy brings a heavy-duty responsibility to a bartender. His Woolf Barnato has him off to a good start, though. Keep it simple. That's the key."

"So there are people who actually care who invented particular drinks, Professor?"

"Of course there are, David. I know folk who spend hours and hours arguing about who created the Manhattan."

"And the answer is ...?"

"We don't know. The closest we've come so far is that it was 'a man named Black' who ran a joint in Manhattan in the 1860s."

"Dear me, how frustrating for you," says David with a roll of his eyes. "You should probably make a note of this new Savoy chappie's name lest frustration drives someone to insanity in the next century ..."

Woolf Barnato

Adapted from a recipe created by Salim Khoury, head barman in the American Bar at London's Savoy Hotel, 2003.

10 ml (.3 oz) vodka

10 ml (.3 oz) peach schnapps

10 ml (.3 oz) blue curaçao

Chilled champagne

Pour the vodka, schnapps, and curaçao into a chilled champagne flute. Top with the champagne.

The Bentley Cocktail

Adapted from a recipe in *The Savoy Cocktail Book*, 1930.

45 ml (1.5 oz) calvados or apple brandy

45 ml (1.5 oz) Dubonnet Rouge

1 lemon twist, as garnish

Stir the calvados and the Dubonnet over ice and strain into
a chilled cocktail glass. Add the garnish.

A Word at the End of the Bar

'm not sure what spurred this story, though I'll bet that my friend Stephan Wilkinson, writer of books and magazine pieces on cars, airplanes, and other manly subjects, had something to do with this. Although he's leading a quieter lifestyle these days, time was when Stephan always seemed to be jetting all over the world to test drive the new "insert flash car of your choice here," and I actually accompanied him for one of his drives back in the nineties. He picked up next year's model of a fabulous sports car, and he and I went distillery hopping in Kentucky for a few days. Grand trip, that was.

Episode 27

Tom and Jerry

THE COCKTAILIAN CHRONICLES

The Professor, our cocktailian bartender, is taking a day off work to celebrate the New Year, but he isn't taking a break from mixing drinks. He and his partner are throwing a party.

"Donna tells me that Lesley is now afraid of eggs. She raises chickens, too . . . How can we get her to drink a Tom and Jerry?" The Professor asks, as he sips from his first cup of coffee of the day.

Lesley isn't actually afraid of eggs, she's afraid of getting salmonella poisoning from the raw eggs that The Professor must use to make this traditional holiday-time drink. Tom and Jerry is akin to eggnog, but far lighter in texture, and very flavorful.

"Calm down, dear, we can get pasteurized shell eggs now, remember?"

The Professor's face lights up. Pasteurized shell eggs, as opposed to any other form of pasteurized eggs, look exactly like those plucked from right under a chicken, and there's no chance of contracting salmonella poisoning from them.

"Jerry Thomas, the nineteenth-century barkeep I'm always talking about, refused to serve Tom and Jerry before the first snowfall of the year. Dontcha love a cantankerous bartender?" asks The Professor.

"Kinda goes without saying…" his partner answers, with a mischievous grin.

It's almost time for the guests to arrive, and The Professor is making the first batch of Tom and Jerrys. He's glancing out of the window every 20 seconds or so, praying for a few freaky flakes of snow to fall. His partner catches him.

"Fat chance, Professor—last time Fog City saw an inch of snow was 1976. I'll take the coats if you serve the drinks."

The doorbell rings and various and sundry friends begin to arrive. The Professor hesitates and takes one last, wistful glance toward the window, but before he has a chance to pour the first drink, a voice bellows from the back of the crowd:

"Hold on, Professor. You're gonna need this."

The Professor looks up to see his pal Stuffy tossing something through the air to him. He catches it deftly, looks at the gift, and smiles large, shaking his new snow globe of the Golden Gate bridge.

Tom and Jerry

Makes about 24 six-ounce drinks

12 pasteurized eggs, separated

300 g (1.5 cups) sugar

1 teaspoon baking soda

2.16L (72 oz or 9 cups) milk

720 ml (24 oz or 3 cups) añejo rum

180 ml (6 oz or .75 cup) brandy

Freshly grated nutmeg, as garnish

1. In a mixing bowl, combine the egg yolks, 250 g (1.25 cups) of the sugar, and the baking soda. Whisk until the mixture is creamy and thick.

2. Pour the milk into a large saucepan over moderate heat. Warm the milk until bubbles form around the edges of the pan and the milk is steaming hot.

3. Very gradually add some of the hot milk to the egg yolk mixture to warm it. Whisk continuously until all of the milk is incorporated. Pour the mixture back into the saucepan and set it over low heat. Cook, whisking constantly, until the mixture thickens just enough to lightly coat a spoon or until a thermometer reaches 160 to 165°F. Remove the pan from the heat and continue whisking for 2 minutes.

4. Stir in the rum and brandy.

5. In a clean mixing bowl, beat the egg whites until frothy. Sprinkle on the remaining 50 g (.25 cup) sugar and continue

beating until soft peaks form. Fold the egg whites into the batter.

6. Ladle the Tom and Jerrys into Tom and Jerry mugs, and sprinkle each serving with a touch of freshly grated nutmeg.

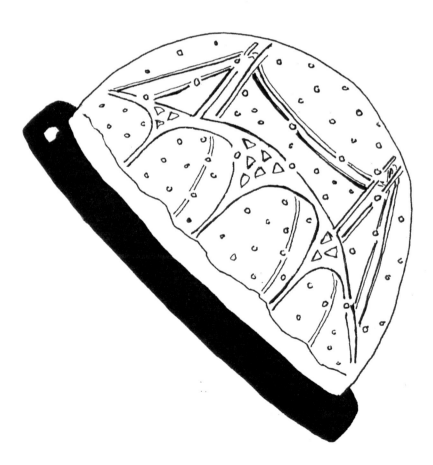

A Word at the End of the Bar

Donna and Lesley are friends of mine, and I guess that Lesley was taking the egg/salmonella scare seriously when I penned this piece. She wasn't alone back then, but according to George Chang, food microbiologist and professor emeritus at U. C. Berkeley, "In studies of clean, intact eggs from modern egg factory facilities, less than 1 percent of the eggs contain detectable salmonella." He went on to say that the risk of salmonella poisoning from eggs is "perhaps even lower than the risk of eating raw salads - definitely lower than the risk of crossing a street against a red light." (Excerpted from *Egg White Cocktails Going Over Easy* by Cindy Lee, Staff Writer, *San Francisco Chronicle*, June 6, 2008.)

Episode 28

21 Hayes

"He named it after a bus, I'm telling you."

"Well, if you say so, Professor, but that's a heck of a lot of work to go through to make a drink that's, admittedly, quite wonderful, only to then go name the darned thing after a bus," declares Wills. Wills is a regular at The Professor's joint who has taught our cocktailian bartender much about cocktails and their various histories.

"Stranger things have happened, Wills—wasn't it you who told me that the Ward Eight was created to celebrate an election victory before the votes had been counted?"

"True enough, Professor. True enough."

Wills had sampled the 21 Hayes Cocktail at the Absinthe Brasserie and Bar about a week before visiting The Professor, and he couldn't get the drink out of his mind. Created by Bar Manager Rob Schwartz, a.k.a. Dr. Schwartz, the 21 Hayes is a gin-based drink, but not just any old gin will suffice. Because one of the ingredients in the drink is cucumber, Schwartz first tried using Hendrick's gin since this bottling is infused with cucumbers, but he found that the "cucumber was overkill," and selected Damrak gin, from Amsterdam, instead. "It turned out to be a great gin to use because it's mild and has nice citrus notes," says Schwartz.

The gin wasn't the only ingredient that fascinated Wills, though. Pimm's No. 1 Cup, an English concoction that's been around since the early 1800s, also caught his eye. Made with a gin base, Pimm's is flavored with fruity liqueurs and plenty of herbs. It's usually served in pint beer mugs, topped with club soda, and garnished with a sliver of cucumber rind. Wills had immense respect for Schwartz's thought processes as he analyzed the drink in his head.

"I had a 21 Hayes not two weeks ago, Wills, and Dr. Schwartz told me that the other special aspect of this drink is that he muddles together some of the cucumber slices with the Pimm's and a few ice cubes when he starts the preparation. Hold on, I wrote down what he told me in my notebook."

The Professor pulls his battered notepad from the drawer behind the bar, leafs back a few pages, and begins to read: "The reason I use the ice while I'm muddling this is I feel it helps give some tooth—it's easier to break down the cucumber, and [it] makes some nice [ice] chips."

"Still, though, he went to all of that trouble, created a great drink, and he had to name the darned thing after a bus," Wills protests.

"Says that the color of the drink is similar to that of the minibuses that pass Absinthe all the time, but he did have a bit of an ulterior motive, too . . ."

"And what was that?"

"His wife's grandmother. First female MUNI driver during WWII."

"Brownie points, huh?"

"Make the world go around, Wills . . ."

21 Hayes

Created by Rob Schwartz, Bar Manager, Absinthe Brasserie and Bar, San Francisco, circa 2004.

3 slices cucumber, about 1/4" thick

7.5 ml (.25 oz) Pimm's No. 1 Cup

45 ml (1.5 oz) gin

7.5 ml (.25 oz) fresh lemon juice

1 splash simple syrup

In a large mixing glass, using a wooden muddler, muddle together 4 or 5 small ice cubes with 2 slices of the cucumber and the Pimm's until the cucumber is almost liquid—some of the skin will be left. Fill the mixing glass two-thirds full of ice, add the gin, lemon juice, and simple syrup. Shake well and strain into a chilled cocktail glass. Garnish with the remaining cucumber slice.

A Word at the End of the Bar

'm still in touch with Rob Schwartz. He moved to the East Coast and works, I think, for a major liquor distributor. We bump into each other at various and sundry liquor related events where we raise out glasses and toast San Franciscan buses. Or something like that.

Episode 29

Kumquat Caipiroshka

It's Tuesday afternoon and the usual group of bartenders have gathered at The Professor's joint to discuss cocktails, new products, and anything else they can think of that's related to the bar business. The Professor rings the bell to get everyone's attention, and after waiting a couple of seconds for the talking to die down, he yells out, "Stick Drinks. How's everyone coping with stick drinks?"

Not everyone at the bar knows exactly what The Professor is talking about, but he is referring to a style of drink that calls for some ingredients to be muddled together with a wooden muddler—or stick. Enrico's restaurant, on Broadway at Kearny, features quite a variety of this style of drink, and The Professor first heard the term, "stick drinks," from David Nepove, the Bar Manager there.

The assembled mass get into a long discussion about stick drinks such as the Mojito and the Caipirinha—both very popular over the past few years—and The Professor advises everyone to use granulated sugar, as opposed to simple syrup, if they are muddling ingredients together.

"Especially if you're muddling lemons, limes, and oranges—the sugar will abrade the zest of the fruit, and this will bring out the flavors of the essential oils that lurk there," he tells them.

The door opens and Regina, the raunchy waitress, strolls into the bar and joins the group. She doesn't often attend these unofficial meetings, but when she does, she's almost certain to cause some sort of trouble. The Professor ignores her and tells the group that now is the time to get Kumquat Caipiroshkas at Enrico's. Kumquats have a relatively short season, so the drink isn't always available there.

"Dave Nepove had special muddlers made for him," Regina tells the group. "They're about twice the size as most."

"That's true," confirms The Professor, "and I love the fact that he chose a citrus vodka for his Kumquat Caipiroshka—the flavors works incredibly well together."

"Especially if you use a king-sized muddler," chirps Regina.

The Professor ignores her again.

The afternoon is drawing to a close, and most of the bartenders have headed off to start their night shifts, but one or two are lingering at the bar.

"I'll have to get to Enrico's and try some of these drinks," says Jen, a local bartender.

"I'll come with you, but I'm not keen on kumquats," says Regina.

"So why go?" The Professor asks.

"Oh, it will be worth the trip just to watch David working with those custom-made muddlers . . ."

Kumquat Caipiroshka

Created by David Nepove, Bar Manager, Enrico's, San Francisco, circa 2004.

5 kumquats

2 teaspoons granulated sugar

60 ml (2 oz) Skyy Citrus vodka

In a large mixing glass, using a wooden muddler, muddle together 4 or 5 small ice cubes with the kumquats and the sugar until the fruit is entirely pulverized. Fill the mixing glass two-thirds full of ice, add the vodka, and shake. Pour (do not strain) into a 10-ounce tumbler or a large old-fashioned glass.

A Word at the End of the Bar

Like Rob Schwartz of the 21 Hayes Cocktail fame, David Nepove now works for a major liquor distributor, and he also has his own line of muddlers—you can find them at mister-mojito.com. I spent time in Mexico with David a few years ago, and I have to say that he's a grand lad to have with you on a tequila-laden trip. He's a tall guy—well over six feet—and by the looks of him he works out at the gym for about seventeen hours a day. I kept telling our traveling companions that if he started any trouble they should reach out to me, and I'd take care of him. Same goes for you, dear reader. If David Nepove gives you any trouble, come find me. I'll show you where to hide . . .

Episode 30

The Horseshoe Sling

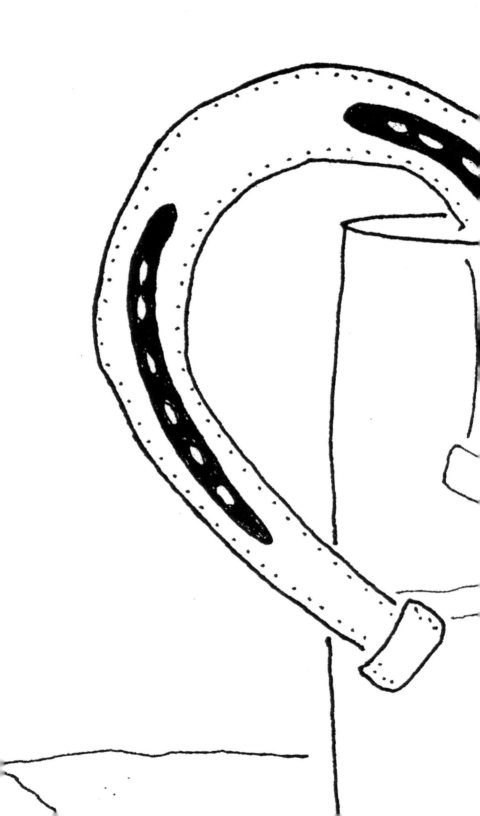

"**S**ingapore Sling? Jeez, it's been years since anyone ordered a Singapore Sling. How do you like it?"

The stranger at The Professor's bar shoots our cocktailian bartender a question with his eyes. "I dunno. My favorite bartender back home makes them for me all the time. I don't ask questions. Just put my money on the bar, keep myself to myself, drink 'em, and go home. What's the problem?"

"No real problem, it's just that nobody's really sure what the original recipe was, so it's one of those debatable drinks. People tend to have their preferences when it comes to the ingredients. Presume you want a gin base, though?"

"That's right. Just like they make it at the Raffles Hotel where it was created."

"You take cherry brandy?"

"Wouldn't be pink without cherry brandy, would it?"

"Depends on what kind of cherry brandy you use."

The Singapore Sling, according to the Raffles Hotel in Singapore, is made with gin, Bénédictine, Cointreau, Cherry

Heering—a proprietary liqueur, sweet and red—pineapple juice, lime juice, Angostura bitters, and club soda. Cocktail freak Ted Haigh, though, known in some circles as Dr. Cocktail, thinks that the drink could have been derived from the Straights Sling, another Singapore creation that called for dry cherry brandy, an eau de vie that's usually served chilled as a post-prandial potion.

"Tell you what," says The Professor, "I've always wanted to make a variation on this drink. Give me a little leeway and if you don't like it, it's on the house."

"Deal," says the stranger. The Professor reaches for a bottle of tequila.

Tequila tastes nothing like gin, but The Professor believes that there are similarities between these two spirits. Both are complex: gin because of the array of botanicals infused or distilled into it; tequila because the agave, the Mexican member of the amaryllis family from which it's made, produces an abundance of vegetal flavors that might not mimic gin, but remind The Professor of gin all the same. He makes the drink and places it on the bar. The stranger takes a sip.

"It ain't a Singapore Sling, but that's surely a great drink," he says. "Got a name for it?"

The Professor looks at the bottle of tequila he used. Herradura Silver, a high-end, 100-percent agave bottling that displays the full array of agave flavors. Other highly regarded 100-percent agave bottlings of tequila include Cazadores Reposado, Chinaco, Jose Cuervo Traditional, Don Eduardo, Don Julio, Patron, Sauza Hornitos Reposado, and El Tesoro. The Herradura la-

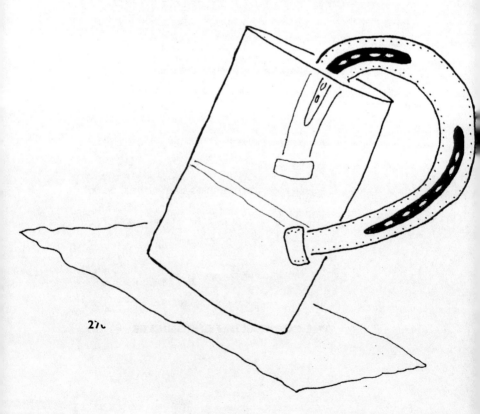

bel uses a horseshoe as its trademark logo. "Call it a Horseshoe Sling," he says.

"Drinking in this joint can be hard work," the stranger comments.

"Come back when I'm busy—that's when you'll find me slinging slings with no questions asked."

The Horseshoe Sling

60 ml (2 oz) Herradura Silver 100-percent Blue Agave tequila

22.5 ml (.75 oz) fresh lime juice

7.5 ml (.25 oz) Bénédictine

7.5 ml (.25 oz) Cherry Heering

15 ml (.5 oz) Cointreau

7.5 ml (.25 oz) pineapple juice

2 dashes Angostura bitters

Club soda (or chilled sparkling wine)

1 lime wedge, as garnish

1 orange wheel, as garnish

Shake and strain the tequila, lime juice, Bénédictine, Cherry Heering, Cointreau, pineapple juice, and bitters over ice. Strain into a tall, ice-filled collins glass. Top with the club soda or chilled sparkling wine. Add the garnishes.

A Word at the End of the Bar

This simple variation on the Singapore Sling, which works very well indeed, was a drink that we came up with at "Cocktails in the Country," the series of bartender workshops I held at my local joint, Painter's, in the Hudson Valley. I've lifted the following from *the bartender's GIN compendium*, my 2009 book, and it will probably give you more info than you ever wanted on the Singapore Sling:

Singapore Sling: A Discussion

The Singapore Sling is one of those drinks that's long been the topic of debate among bartenders in the wee hours of the morning, and it's probably caused a couple of fisticuff battles, too. It wasn't long ago that we all believed that the Raffles Hotel version was the one and only real McCoy, but then that pesky Ted "Dr. Cocktail" Haigh came along, did a little more research than the rest of us, and deduced that the very first Singapore Sling might have been made with kirschwasser—a cherry eau de vie—instead of the Heering cherry liqueur that we find in most recipes. Eau de vie, for the record, is a distilled spirit, and liqueurs are distilled spirits that have been sweetened and flavored with various botanical ingredients—these are vastly different products.

David Embury, it seems, agree with Doc. In the second edition of *The Fine Art of Mixing Drinks*—I haven't seen a first edition—he calls specifically for kirsch in his Singapore Gin Sling, stating, "Of all the recipes published for this drink I have never seen any two that were alike." Embury calls for gin, simple syrup, lemon or lime juice, kirsch, and a dash of Angostura, then adds that "some recipes call for the addition of a pony of Bénédictine."

Next up we have George Sinclair, the Thinking Bartender, and his nicely-researched article about this drink led me to look again at *The Gentleman's Companion* by

Charles H. Baker Jr., 1939. Here we have yet another version, this one named "The Immortal Singapore Raffles Gin Sling" in Baker's book. This formula is somewhat minimalist, and a little on the sweet side, but it's good to record these things, right?

Here, then, are three versions of this drink. The first is said to have been created in the early 1900s at the Raffles Hotel in Singapore by bartender Ngiam Tong Boon, and the second receipt is based on the formula uncovered by Dr. Cocktail in a book dating to 1922—Haigh's discovery was called the Straights Sling, but it was referred to as a "well-known Singapore drink"—and the third recipe is based on Baker's book.

Singapore Sling (Raffles Hotel Style)

The ingredients in this version are listed on a coaster from the Raffles Hotel, but no measurements were given, and the club soda isn't mentioned.

60 ml (2 oz) Beefeater gin

15 ml (.5 oz) Cherry Heering

7.5 ml (.25 oz) Bénédictine

15 ml (.5 oz) Cointreau

60 ml (2 oz) pineapple juice

20 ml (.75 oz) fresh lime juice

2 dashes Angostura bitters

Club soda

Shake everything except the club soda and strain into an ice-filled collins glass. Top with club soda.

Singapore Sling (Straights Sling Style)

Adapted from a recipe for a "Straights Sling" found by Ted "Dr. Cocktail" Haigh in a book published in 1922. This is a dry version of the drink that calls for kirsch, a cherry eau de vie, instead of a sweetened cherry brandy.

60 ml (2 oz) gin

15 ml (.5 oz) Bénédictine

15 ml (.5 oz) kirschwasser

22.5 ml (.75 oz) fresh lemon juice

2 dashes orange bitters

2 dashes Angostura bitters

Club soda

Shake everything except the club soda and strain into an ice-filled collins glass. Top with club soda.

Singapore Sling (Charles H. Baker Style)

The Immortal Singapore Raffles Gin Sling, Met in 1926, and thereafter Never Forgotten . . . The original formula is 1/3 each of dry gin, cherry brandy and Bénédictine; shake it for a moment, or stir it in a barglass, with 2 fairly large lumps of ice to chill. Turn into a small 10 oz highball glass with one lump of ice left in and fill up to individual taste with chilled club soda. Garnish with the spiral peel of 1 green lime. In other ports in the Orient drinkers often use C & C ginger ale instead of soda, or even stone bottle ginger beer." *The Gentleman's Companion* by Charles H. Baker Jr., 1939.

30 ml (1 oz) dry gin
30 ml (1 oz) cherry brandy
30 ml (1 oz) Bénédictine
Club soda, ginger ale, or ginger beer
1 lime spiral, as garnish

Shake the gin, cherry brandy, and the Bénédictine over ice, strain into an ice-filled highball or collins glass, top with the soda, and add the garnish.

Episode 31

The Ruby Delicious

The Professor, our cocktailian bartender, is clearing away the placemat, napkin, and assorted crockery and cutlery in front of Salvatore. A quiet guy who almost always eats alone at the bar, Salvatore has just finished his lunch.

"That was great, Professor, but I might have eaten a little too much. You got a digestif to suggest?"

"I don't like recommending drinks for medicinal purposes, but I do know that, in the U.K., people often mix port and brandy together to take the edge off an over-loaded stomach. The drink's known as Port and Brandy—very creative those Brits, they invented the Gin and Tonic, too. Wanna try the Port and Brandy?"

Salvatore, reflecting his usual demeanor, merely smiles and nods.

It's true that Port and Brandy is used by many people in Britain as a potion to quell over-full stomachs, but there's no medical proof to support the fact that it works. There are, however, many first-hand accounts of the success of this drink. Other potions often credited with the same properties include Jägermeister—that's right, it's not just for young people looking to get a little high—Italian amari, or "bitters," such as Fratelli Averna, and Underberg, a German digestif sold in miniature bottles and usually found at ski lodges in the U.S.

The Professor pours equal amounts of ruby port and cognac into a sherry copita glass and places it in front of Salvatore who takes a sip and smiles, as if to say, "That should do the trick." The Professor's mind is working, though. He's wondering if he can use the mixture of port and brandy as a base for a new cocktail.

Looking over the bottles on the backbar, our bartender spots a nonalcoholic apple-flavored syrup that he's been using to add an accent to coffees and teas. Perhaps this will be the component to make the Port and Brandy into a real cocktail. He starts to experiment with various ratios of the three ingredients until he thinks he's arrived at a properly balanced drink. He hands it to Salvatore to sample.

"That's really good, Professor," says his appreciative friend across the mahogany. "It wouldn't work as a digestif, but it could be a winner as a regular cocktail. I think that the apple

syrup gives it a nice sweetness, but the port and brandy make a sturdy backbone for the drink, so it's not too sweet. Probably not a drink for Dry Gin Martini lovers, but I'll bet the majority of your customers would like it."

The Professor beams, and he's astonished to hear so many words issue forth from Salvatore's mouth. He decides to push the issue.

"Are you really sure it's not too sweet, Salvatore? I could cut back on the apple syrup a little. Or maybe increase the brandy just a tad? What do you think? Should I try another version?"

"Check, please, Professor," says Salvatore.

"Is it something I said?"

"No, it's just that I'm meeting people for dinner tonight."

"And ...?"

"And I'm almost out of words for the day."

The Ruby Delicious

60 ml (2 oz) cognac
60 ml (2 oz) ruby port
45 ml (1.5 oz) Monin apple syrup
1 apple slice, as garnish
Stir the ingredients over ice and strain into a chilled cocktail glass. Add the garnish.

A Word at the End of the Bar

The man called Salvatore in this piece is based on Salvatore Buttiglierri, co-owner with his brother Peter, of Painter's, my local joint. These guys have been like brothers to me, and I'll take up space in this book to tell 'em I love 'em both dearly. And yes, Sal is a pretty quiet guy, and the sentence, "I'm almost out of words for the day," did spew forth from his lips one evening at Painter's.

The Ruby Delicious works pretty well, though I'm a far bigger fan of Port and Brandy, and at the time of writing (February, 2010), I've had exactly that drink for my nightcap for the last two nights. Wanna hear a dirty little secret? I made both drinks with Warre's Vintage 1977 porto (bottled in 1979), and Hennessy Paradis cognac.

They were fuckin' fabulous!

Episode 32

The McEwan

The Professor, our cocktailian bartender, is busy arguing with one of his regular customers about the characteristics of single malt scotches.

"I'm telling you, Professor, you let me taste any of your scotches, I'll tell you which general area of Scotland it comes from," says Bruce, an arrogant young man who's been tutoring himself on the subject for about six months.

"Would you like to put some money behind that statement?" The Professor asks.

"Tell you what. I'll pay for each dram I get wrong. You pay if I get it right."

"Deal. Now turn away from the bar and I'll set up a flight of three scotches for you.

First The Professor pours a shot of a Lowland malt, Auchentoshen Three Wood. Although Lowland whiskies are generally characterized as being soft and a little on the light side, this one has been aged in bourbon casks and two kinds of sherry butts—the result is a sweet and fruity dram that's almost cognac-like in nature.

Next he pours from a bottle of 15-year-old Glenmorangie, a Northern Highland malt that has more salty notes than any of the other Glenmorangie bottlings and a hint of leather that's unusual for a whisky from this distillery. And finally, The Professor pours a dram from a bottle of 10-year-old Bruichladdich, a whisky from the island of Islay, an area known for producing the peatiest drams in Scotland. But that isn't the case with Bruichladdich—there's barely any peat to be found in this scotch at all.

"You can turn around now," The Professor tells Bruce, presenting the flight of whiskies, complete with spring water and crackers for palate cleansing. Bruce samples all three, deliberating after each one, and naming the area from which he thinks it hails. He pins the Auchentoshen Three Wood down as a western Highland whisky, since it reminds him a little of the Glendronach; the Glenmorangie 15-year-old is picked as being a Campbelltown malt, because of the wonderful saltiness that's characteristic of whiskies from this west-coast town, and the Bruichladdich simply confounds him.

"It's bright, fresh, floral, and even a little fruity, too. I'll say it's a Speyside malt, but I'm really guessing on this one," Bruce confesses. Speyside is an area of the Scottish Highlands known for producing superlative malts in many differing styles.

The door opens and in walks a man in a kilt. He strides to the mahogany and begins to peruse the bottles behind the bar. The Professor gives him a nod to let him know that he's been noticed and proceeds to tell Bruce that he'd been wrong about all three whiskies.

"Is this a blind tasting, then?" asks the kilted stranger, his Scottish brogue clearly evident.

"It is indeed," The Professor tells him. "Would you like to take your chances?"

The Scot names all three specific bottlings immediately after tasting each one, and adds, "Jacques Bezuidenhout, from the Irish Bank on Mark Lane, has made a nice little cocktail out of that Bruichladdich—we call it The Laddie at work, and Jacques' drink is called The McEwan—ye should go try one when you're in the neighborhood."

The Professor holds out his hand, and the Scot takes it with a hearty shake.

"They call me The Professor."

"Aye, so I've heard. They call me Jim McEwan. I sort of work at the Bruichladdich distillery. Just popped in to make sure

you were carrying the good stuff. I believe you hand out scotch on the house if someone passes your test?"

The Professor nods.

"There's no better way for a Scot to start the day," he grins.

The McEwan

Adapted from a recipe by Jacques Bezuidenhuit, The Irish Bank, San Francisco.

60 ml (2 oz) Bruichladdich 10-year-old single malt scotch

7.5 ml (.25 oz) Poire William eau de vie

15 ml (.5 oz) fresh lemon juice

15 ml (.5 oz) clove and cinnamon simple syrup

1 teaspoon raw egg white (optional)

Freshly grated nutmeg, as garnish

Shake all of the ingredients over ice. Strain into an ice-filled old-fashioned glass. Add the garnish.

Clove and Cinnamon Simple Syrup

Adapted from a recipe by Jacques Bezuidenhuit, The Irish Bank, San Francisco.

600 ml (20 oz or 2.5 cups) hot water

500 g (2.5 cups) granulated sugar

2 cinnamon sticks, broken into 2-inch pieces

30 whole cloves

Combine the water and the sugar in a saucepan and cook, stirring frequently, over moderate heat, until the sugar dissolves. Reduce the heat and add the cinnamon sticks and cloves. Simmer for ten minutes. Let cool to room temperature. Bottle and refrigerate.

A Word at the End of the Bar

Jim McEwan is another dear old friend of mine, and I think that he'd just left Bowmore to join the Bruichladdich distillery when this column was published. And although I don't go back quite so far with Jacques Bezuidenhuit as I do with Jim, Jacques is a dear old friend, too. He currently works for the Kimpton Hotel chain, and he's one of the most respected cocktailians in the business.

This column reminded me of another drink that I created one night when I was tending bar at Painter's. In 2004 and 2005, I held occasional "happenings" at Painter's. The events were called *organized chaos*, and they took place in the Gallery Bar, a small lounge that's usually used for private parties. I was allowed to do what the heck I wanted when I held these things, so I played my music—sixties and seventies rock and roll with some punk thrown in there, and some hokey numbers such as *Que Sera, Sera*, thrown in there, too. I served good cocktails at *organized chaos*, and the regulars were very appreciative. We had some great nights.

One night I noticed three woodworkers—master craftsmen— having a conversation at the end of the bar. How often does that happen? I wondered. And that led to me creating the following drink, using the Auchentoshan Three Wood single malt scotch as a base, to commemorate the occasion. It works pretty well.

Three Wood-Workers

75 ml (2.5 oz) Auchentoshan Three Wood single malt scotch

15 ml (.5 oz) maraschino liqueur

15 ml (.5 oz) dark crème de cacao

3 dashes orange bitters

Stir over ice and strain into a chilled cocktail glass

Episode 33

S.O.C.

"**A**s I live and breathe, if it isn't Fancy Nancy," says The Professor as a pretty blonde woman sidles up to the bar. "They let you out of Virginia again? Do the Feds know?"

"You, my dear Professor, may now call me Fancy Schmancy Nancy. Jud and I are just back from a cruise around the French Polynesian islands on the *Paul Gauguin*. The bartenders on board the ship treated me with respect. You should try it sometime."

"Don't tell me you started tipping, Nancy."

"Not allowed on board that ship. They just know how to treat a lady, that's all."

Nancy grins, leans over the bar, and gives The Professor a big kiss on the cheek. The Professor smiles large, too. It's been years since he's seen Nancy, though she used to visit the city often.

"So where's Jud?"

"He's shopping for new sandals, but he should be here soon. Ruined his old ones walking on the coral in the South Pacific. Did I mention we're just back from Tahiti?"

"Not specifically, Nancy, but I get the picture. You wanna glass of waht wahn?" The Professor tries, unsuccessfully, to mimic Nancy's Southern drawl—white wine has always been Nancy's drink of choice.

"No sir. Fancy Schmancy Nancy is a cocktail girl. I'll take an S.O.C., if you don't mind."

"Okay, Nancy. What does S.O.C. stand for?"

"No idea, Professor. Jonathan Abogado, the bartender at the Connoisseur's Club, on the cruise ship I was mentioning? Well, he comes from the Philippines, and he told me that the words in his language translate to 'pretty lady, come to me.' It's his own creation, you know."

"And the ingredients are . . . ?"

"Well, now, I did take note. I figured I couldn't expect you to know every drink under the sun. It's made with cognac, Chambord, and Frangelico. He shakes it up real nice, and strains it into a big ol' cocktail glass."

"I get the picture, Nancy. Let me see what I can do."

Chambord is a French cordial made from black raspberries, and Frangelico, from Italy, is flavored with hazelnuts. Mixed with cream, half-and-half, or milk, these two liqueurs are used to make a drink known as Nuts and Berries, and some people use an Irish cream liqueur instead of the cream, adding some chocolate notes to the drink.

The Professor uses the cognac as the base of Nancy's drink, and sweetens the brandy by using both liqueurs in equal quantities. He pauses for a second, then picks up a bottle of Angostura bitters to add a touch of complexity, stirs the combination over ice, strains it into a champagne flute, and twists a wide piece of lemon peel over the top of the glass.

Nancy loves her cocktail, and twenty minutes later she's about to order another one when the door opens and Jud, her husband, walks in.

"Jud! The Professor fixed me a cocktail like the ones I drank on board the ship." She turns to The Professor. "Maybe just one more …?" But Jud intervenes. "Sorry, Nancy, but I've arranged to meet Eric and Caroline in just over an hour. We really should get back to the hotel and start getting ready," he tells her.

"Not just one more little itsy-bitsy cocktail, Jud?"

"I don't think so, Nancy. S.O.C., babe, S.O.C."

S.O.C.

Adapted from a recipe by Jonathan Abogado, bartender on the Radisson Seven Seas cruise ship *Paul Gauguin*, sailing out of Tahiti.

75 ml (2.5 oz) cognac

22.5 ml (.75 oz) Chambord

22.5 ml (.75 oz) Frangelico

2 dashes Angostura bitters (optional)

1 lemon twist, as garnish

Stir all of the ingredients over ice for 20 to 30 seconds. Strain into a chilled champagne flute or cocktail glass, and add the garnish.

A Word at the End of the Bar

Mardee and I met Jud, Nancy, Eric, and Caroline on a cruise around the French Polynesian islands on the *Paul Gauguin* in 2004, and that's where I found this drink. I'd gone through major surgery followed by intensive radiation in late 2003, and the cruise was an attempt to "put all that behind me." To be quite honest, the whole trip is a little fuzzy in my memory.

Strange days, indeed.

Episode 34

Peachy Keen

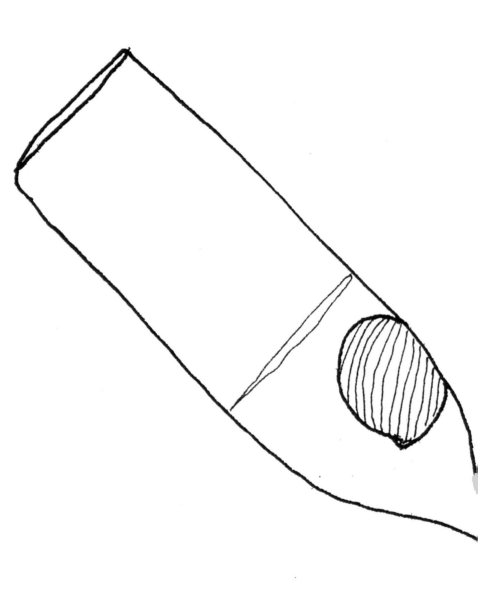

"**P**rofessor, since I'm the only one at the bar this afternoon, I wonder if you'd do me the favor of playing this CD?" Doc, a regular at The Professor's bar, is making the request. The Professor takes the CD from his hand and peruses its cover.

"Could you give me about 20 minutes, Doc?"

"Any particular reason?"

"Yeah. You haven't taken it out of its wrapping yet."

"Oh, Professor. Give it back and hand me your fruit knife."

Two minutes later The Professor is playing the CD, and although he's not really a fan of country music, Robert Earl Keen's **Farm Fresh Onions** album makes him smile.

"This guy's got a really distinctive voice. Never heard him sing before, but I did have the cocktail named for him when I was down in Texas last year," he tells Doc.

"Does everything have to be about cocktails, Professor?"

"Ever notice I'm a bartender?"

"Okay, okay. Please tell me about this drink."

"It comes from John Sheely, a chef who owns the Mockingbird Bistro Wine Bar in Houston. The place has a great reputation—they serve Texan food with a French influence, if you can believe that."

"I've never known you to lie to me before, Professor."

The Professor goes on to explain that Sheely is a big fan of Robert Earl Keen, and in keeping with the French/Texan theme at his restaurant, he uses only French and Texan ingredients to create his tribute to the singer, the Peachy Keen Cocktail. The drink contains Citadelle French vodka, and Mathilde Liqueur Pêches, a French peach liqueur that The Professor considers to be exceptional.

Liqueurs can be made in many ways—sometimes artificial flavorings and colorings are used to produce lower-priced cordials, whereas the better bottlings are made with fresh ingredients. Many top-quality brands are made this way, hence the relatively high prices. The company that makes the Mathilde range of fruit cordials infuses fresh fruits into neutral spirits for as long as

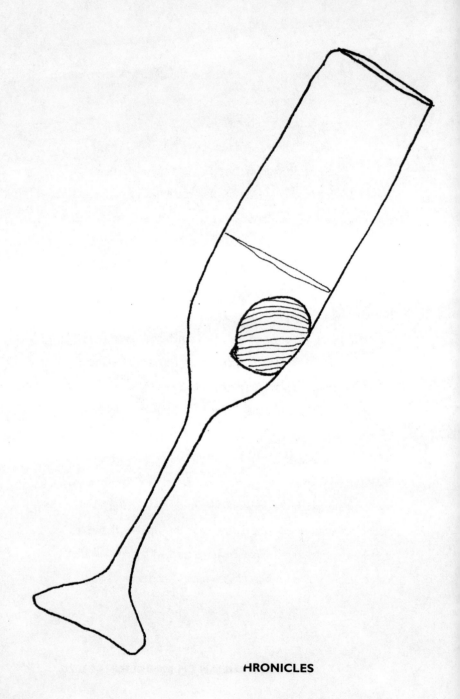

HRONICLES

eight months to extract their natural flavors and color. Mathilde liqueurs are available in a variety of flavors, including cassis (black currants), framboise (raspberries), and poire (pear), all of which are highly recommendable.

"Perhaps you could fix me a Peachy Keen, Professor?"

"Sorry, Doc. I don't have all the ingredients."

"But I know you stock Citadelle vodka, and you carry Cîroc—that's another great vodka from France. As for the Mathilde liqueurs, I can see them right there, behind you."

"It's the garnish I'm all out of—I need a wedge of Texas peach to make the drink properly."

"Oh, Professor, make the cocktail anyway and we'll listen to the title track of Keen's album as a garnish of sorts."

"A Peachy Keen Cocktail with a *Farm Fresh Onion* garnish? I sure hope John Sheely doesn't hear about this ..."

The Peachy Keen

Adapted from a recipe created by John Sheely, The Mockingbird Bistro Wine Bar. Houston, Texas.

45 ml (1.5 oz) Citadelle or Cîroc vodka

30 ml (1 oz) Mathilde Pêche liqueur

I wedge fresh Texas peach, as garnish

Stir the vodka and liqueur over ice for 20 to 30 seconds. Strain into a chilled champagne flute or cocktail glass. Add the garnish.

A Word at the End of the Bar

I can't quite remember how this recipe fell into my hands, but I'm pretty sure that I chose to put it into the Chron because it featured Citadelle vodka and a Mathilde liqueur. Bothe these products come from Gabriel & Andreu, a fabulous French spirits company that issues nothing but the best in a variety of products, including Ferrand Cognac Abel, the finest cognac I ever did taste. Alexandre Gabriel, the guy who heads up this company, is a man who I'm proud to call a friend, and although we aren't in touch all that often, we've had many interesting discussions on the history of the continuous still, the molecular makeup of spirits, and all sorts of fascinating subjects. Well, they're fascinating to us . . . If you'd like to hear about one of our adventures, type this into your browser: http://ardentspirits. com/BehindTheBarPost.aspx?PostID=686

Episode 35

Hpnotiq Breeze

The Professor, our cocktailian bartender, is enjoying a little peace and quiet after a hectic lunchtime rush. Doc, his friend and long-time regular is sitting in his usual spot, his nose buried in an old book, as is his wont, and the only other people to grace the mahogany are two young guys who have recently started frequenting the bar—they are deep in conversation at the far end. As The Professor quietly polishes the liquor bottles on the backbar, he detects an argument brewing between the two newcomers, so he decides to move closer to them and eavesdrop.

"It was Orson Wells, I'm telling you. He played the part from September, 1937, through March, 1938."

"Well I'm here to tell you that it was Frank Readick's voice on the one show with the 'weed of crime' ending."

"Nonsense. Readick left the show in '35."

The guys are arguing about who read the part of Lamont Cranston, a.k.a. The Shadow, on the radio show that ran from 1930 until 1954. This radio phenomenon, based on the magazine series *The Shadow, A Detective Monthly*, gathered an almost cult-like following, and the sinister voice of the main character was known for using melodramatic phrases such as, "the weed of crime bears bitter fruit." The Professor ambles over.

"Who knows what evil lurks in the heart of man?" The Professor says as he approaches the old-time radio aficionados, thinking he's quoting the line that opened the show.

"The hearts of men, Professor. It's the hearts of men," admonishes Alfred, the taller of the two guys, his face growing ruddier by the minute.

"Let's not get too upset," says The Professor. "It was just a radio show after all."

"Oh, don't go down that road, Professor," advises David. "How about you make us another couple of Bay Breezes, and we'll talk about other things?"

"Sounds sound to me, but let me make you Hpnotiq Breezes instead. It's a drink I tried last night at Cliff House."

The Hpnotiq Breeze is the creation of Jaime Wong, Bar Manager at Cliff House on Point Lobos, and although it's merely a variation on the Bay Breeze—white rum with cranberry and pineapple juices—lots of thought went into choosing the ingredients for Wong's new drink.

Having tried, and enjoyed, Bay Breezes made with cognac as the base liquor, Wong used Hypnotiq liqueur in the drink after noting that the aquamarine, tropical-fruit-flavored liqueur is made from both vodka and cognac. Then, since Hpnotiq is low in alcohol, he added a little extra vodka to give the cocktail a "punch." And when it came to cranberry juice, he chose the white variety so as to retain the color of the liqueur in the drink.

The Professor explains Wong's thinking to the radio freaks as he's making the drinks, delving into every detail he can remember Wong telling him last night.

Alfred and David couldn't really care less about how cocktails are created, but they smile and nod at the right moments, and, after taking a sip of their cocktails, thank The Professor for turning them on to the new drink. The Professor smiles

back at them, and wanders up the bar to see if Doc is ready for another drink.

"Who knows what evil lurks in the hearts of bartenders?" asks David.

"The Professor knows," smiles Alfred.

The Hpnotiq Breeze

45 ml (1.5 oz) Hpnotiq liqueur

22.5 ml (.75 oz) vodka

60 ml (2 oz) pineapple juice

60 ml (2 oz) white cranberry juice

1 lemon twist, as garnish

Fill a shaker two-thirds full of ice and add the Hpnotiq, vodka, pineapple juice, and cranberry juice. Shake for approximately 15 seconds and strain the drink into a chilled cocktail glass. Add the garnish.

A Word at the End of the Bar

Hpnotiq, the tropical-fruit flavored liqueur, saved my life when I was hired to create a drink for a new vodka company, and I was given the mandate that the drink must be the same color as the label on the bottle. "It's blue," they told me. It wasn't, it was aquamarine. I had no idea where to turn to make an aquamarine drink so I popped into my liquor store to look around, and lo and behold, there was a bottle of Hpnotiq. It was brand new on the market at the time.

Thinking that anything this color would taste very nasty indeed, I was pleasantly surprised to discover that Hpnotiq, though fairly sweet, didn't have that artificial candy-like flavor that some other tropical-fruit-flavored liqueurs have, and I've supported the brand ever since. Much to the delight of my younger bartender friends who rib me incessantly about my liking for this stuff. Screw 'em, I say. I'm sticking to my guns on this one.

Episode 36

The Creamery

The Boss is really angry at The Professor because he took the whole of last week off work without notifying the management—he simply arranged for two of the other bartenders to cover his shifts and flew out to New York to visit some bartender friends.

"You can't just leave without telling me. Normal people ask their employers when they want time off work. Usually a few weeks in advance."

"Perhaps you'd better employ some normal people, then." The Professor knows he's pushing his luck, but he has a bad case of jet-lag—his flight got in just before midnight last night, and sleep eluded him save for a couple of hours right before he came to work.

The Boss bites his tongue, shakes his head, and disappears to his basement office. The Professor turns to see that the first person to grace the mahogany this morning is already seated, and no doubt he witnessed the confrontation. A dark-haired Irishman with a graying goatee is sitting patiently at the bar as The Professor ambles over to him.

"Could I just get a cup of coffee to start the old heart?"

"Certainly, sir. Would you like to see the lunch menu, too?"

"Yes, I would indeed. Thank you kindly, sir," smiles the Irishman.

The Professor serves the coffee, places a menu in front of his customer, and walks the length of the bar to serve the second customer of the day. Business starts to pick up, and The Professor doesn't have time to dally with anyone—he's far too busy pouring drinks and taking orders for lunch.

The Irishman, a certain Patrick O'Sullivan, is taking a break from the Big Apple where, unbeknown to The Professor, he tends bar at Seppi's, a fine dining restaurant that offers French, Swiss, and Italian food. But despite Seppi's mainland European theme, Patrick stocks the bar with an impressive selection of Irish whiskeys and uses them to create some pretty spectacular cocktails. Patrick orders lunch from The Professor, washes it down with a pint of ale, and asks for an Irish Coffee.

"Make it with the John Power whiskey if you carry it, please."

"And why's that? I usually use Jameson," asks The Professor.

"The Power has a lot of Power—flavor enough to stand up to the coffee. The Jameson I drink on the rocks."

O'Sullivan now has The Professor's attention, and he asks about other brands of Irish whiskey.

"Redbreast is an incredible whiskey for the price—it has a marvelous peachy quality to it. I drink it neat with just a drop of spring water—same way I take my Kilbeggan. Now there's a whiskey with a great edge to it. Highly desirable indeed. Lots of character."

The Irishman goes on to say that he thinks the Bushmills 10-year-old malt whiskey is great value for money, and that he likes to sip Knappogue Castle, another Irish malt, on the rocks.

"It's a lightish whiskey, but it carries ice well," he says.

"You a drinker or a bartender?" ask The Professor.

O'Sullivan fills him in on his gig in New York, and tells him about a cocktail he created called The Creamery. The Professor, of course, has to make this drink immediately, and he's taking his first sip when the Boss appears at the bar.

"Drinking on the job, Professor?"

"Boss! Meet Patrick O'Sullivan. He's a bartender in New York."

"You one of the guys The Professor flew out to see last week?" asks the Boss.

"Not at all. We just met today, but I've just convinced him to come back east again next week," says Patrick, wearing a straight face.

The Boss's face reddens. He glares at The Professor, but his bartender simply smiles and walks down the bar to pull a beer for a new customer. The Boss storms out of the front door, and The Professor walks back to shake Patrick's hand.

"Very nice, Patrick," he grins.

"I've had bosses like that in my past, too. It's important to know how to get them out of the bar as often as possible."

The Creamery

Created by Patrick O'Sullivan, bartender, Seppi's, New York, circa 2004.

45 ml (1.5 oz) Jameson Irish whiskey

30 ml (1 oz) Kahlúa

15 ml (.5 oz) crème de banane

30 ml (1 oz) heavy cream

Fill a shaker two-thirds full of ice and add all of the ingredients. Shake for approximately 15 seconds and strain the drink into a chilled cocktail glass.

A Word at the End of the Bar

Patrick O'Sullivan is a friend of mine who knows his Irish whiskeys back to front, and at the time of writing Seppi's has just closed its doors after a fabulous 12-year run, so he's taking a well-deserved break right now.

A certain famous person who shall remain nameless went to see Patrick at Seppi's after he read this column when it appeared in the *San Francisco Chronicle*, and he and Patrick remain friends to this day. I'd be amiss if I didn't mention Shelley Clark here, too—she's a marketing maven in Manhattan whom I've known for many years,, and she's been putting up with Patrick as her partner for a good long time now.

I had The Creamery on my cocktail list at Painter's when I held my *organized chaos* sessions. It sold well. And I knocked one all over one of my customers one night, too. Thanks for being so damned nice about it, John!

Episode 37

The Kentucky Mojito
& The Mexican Mojito

"**Y**ou can't call it a Mojito if it's made with bourbon. It's just not right, I'm telling you." Linda, a regular who would frequent The Professor's joint more often if her job would allow her the time, is taking our cocktailian bartender to task about a new drink he's offering.

"But it's okay to call a drink made with vodka and white crème de cacao a Chocolate Martini?" The Professor fires back.

"That's almost as bad, but at least the word 'chocolate' qualifies the name." Linda is a wordsmith by trade.

"And this drink is a 'Kentucky' Mojito. You expect to get rum in a drink from Kentucky?

"Sorry, Professor, but this is just a marketing ploy. Mojitos are hot, so everyone wants in on the act," she points out.

Linda has a good point. The Bay Breeze is an excellent example of a spirits company altering an ingredient in a popular drink— originally made with rum, cranberry juice, and pineapple juice—in order to promote its product. Cleverly, one company substituted its brand of vodka for the rum, and the result was so successful that the majority of bartenders now make the drink with vodka.

In the case of the Kentucky Mojito, though, The Professor believes that this is a legitimate name for the drink. The single aspect of this cocktail that intrigues The Professor most is that it calls for a style of Madeira known as "Rainwater." Rainwater is a light, versatile version of this fortified wine, not as dry as Sercial, which is suitable as an apéritif, or Verdelho, a medium-dry bottling with fairly high acidity. Bual Madeira is medium-sweet and suitable to be served after dinner, and the final style of Madeira available is Malmsey, a sweet wine that fares well alongside chocolate desserts. Madeiras, which have a long shelf life even after being opened, are seldom used as cocktail ingredients.

"Here you go, Linda," says The Professor, placing a tall drink, garnished with fresh mint sprigs, on a coaster in front of her. "The Kentucky Mojito. On the house."

"Okay, I'll try it," sighs Linda. "Which bourbon did you use?"

"Mark Czechowski, the creator, called for Maker's Mark, so that's how I made it. You could try using Old Fitzgerald, Rebel

Yell, Van Winkle, or W. L. Weller. Like Maker's, they're all made with wheat as a tertiary grain, rather than the more traditional rye."

Linda sips her drink as she listens to The Professor. "Well, I must admit that this is a refreshing quaff," she says. "Perhaps tomorrow you could prepare one of these drinks for me?" Linda pulls a folded sheet of paper from her pocket and hands it across the bar. She puts enough money on the mahogany to cover her tab and a generous tip, smiles, and walks out of the bar. The Professor opens the piece of paper, reads the recipe printed on it, and slaps his forehead.

"What's the drink, Professor?" asks the Boss, who has been listening to the banter at the bar.

"She got me fair and square," says The Professor. "It's a recipe for a Tequila Mojito."

"Consider your chain well and truly yanked, Professor."

The Kentucky Mojito

Adapted from a recipe by Mark Czechowski, mixologist at Manhattan's Noche restaurant.

60 ml (2 oz) Maker's Mark bourbon

15 ml (.5 oz) Rainwater Madeira

4 to 6 fresh mint leaves

105 ml (3.5 oz) lemon-lime soda

15 ml (.5 oz) club soda

2 to 3 mint sprigs, as garnish

Put the bourbon, Madeira, and mint leaves into an empty mixing glass and grind them with a wooden muddler until the mint leaves break into flecks. Pour into an ice-filled collins glass, and add the lemon-lime soda and the club soda. Stir briefly. Add the garnish.

The Mexican Mojito

Adapted from a recipe by Dave Singh, Ambassador for Gran Centenario tequila.

45 ml (1.5 oz) Gran Centenario plata tequila

2 teaspoons granulated sugar

6 to 8 fresh mint leaves

Club soda

1 to 2 dashes Angostura bitters

2 to 3 mint sprigs, as garnish

Put the tequila, sugar, and mint leaves into an empty mixing glass and grind them with a wooden muddler until the mint leaves break into flecks. Pour into an ice-filled collins glass, and add the club soda and bitters, and stir briefly. Add the garnish.

A Word at the End of the Bar

I can't for the life of me remember who the heck Linda was in this story, but I'm always arguing with purists who just don't understand that English is constantly evolving, and in the twenty-first century it's evolving fast and hard. You can call a drink whatever you want to call it, as far as I'm concerned, just so long as you're not trying to pull the wool over anyone's eyes. The Kentucky Mojito, by the by, is a really refreshing quaff.

Episode 38

The Rose

Five local bartenders are gathered at The Professor's bar for their weekly discussion of new and noteworthy cocktails and ingredients, and this week they are joined by Dave Wondrich, author of *Esquire Drinks* and cocktail consultant extraordinaire. This isn't Dave's first time in the bar, but he's never been to one of these meetings before. Today he just happened to stumble in at the right time.

"So what does everyone think? Are pink drinks still in vogue?" asks The Professor.

Everyone nods.

"The cranberry juice industry must love whoever came up with the Cosmopolitan," says Jen. "And while we're on that subject, who did invent that drink?"

"Nobody really knows," says The Professor. "Probably someone at Cointreau, but at least they had the decency to formulate a well-balanced cocktail."

Dave Wondrich chimes in, "I just put a new pink drink onto the cocktail list at 5 Ninth, a new joint in Manhattan's Meatpacking District. If you count around 80 years old as being new, that is."

He goes on to tell them about The Rose, a drink that Dave believes was popular in the 1920s and was supposedly created by Johnny Mitta, a guy who tended bar at the Chatham Hotel in Paris. Mitta's joint was close to Harry's New York Bar where famed bartender Harry McElhone held forth from behind the stick.

"I found the recipe in one of McElhone's early books—it was one of those few times that spending hours poring over old cocktail books really paid off. It's a strange formula, though: dry vermouth, kirsch or kirschwasser, and raspberry syrup. In France they used redcurrant syrup, but that's just too hard to find here." He gives The Professor instructions on how to make the drink, and our cocktailian bartender goes to work.

Kirschwasser, a clear eau de vie made from cherries, is an ingredient not used in many cocktail recipes, but it works wonderfully in this drink. Wondrich likes to use the Trimbach bottling from Alsace, but other great renditions of this spirit are available from companies such as Etter, a Swiss entity and the Clear Creek

Distillery in Oregon. St. George Spirits in Alameda, California, renders a kirsch under its Aqua Perfecta label.

"The trick to this cocktail is to go very easy on the raspberry syrup, Professor," Wondrich says as the drink is being built. "And you need to use twice as much vermouth—I use Noilly Prat—as kirschwasser. You'll still get the bite of the eau de vie, but the vermouth will soothe its soul. The sweetness of the raspberry syrup should be just barely detectable at the back of the throat."

The Professor strains the drink into a chilled champagne flute and takes a sip.

"This is heavenly, Dave. This is one of the best cocktails I've ever tasted."

"Why, thank you, sir. You gonna put it on your cocktail list?"

"Yes, but I already have a drink name The Rose on there. Do you think I could change its name?"

"I hate to be obvious, Professor," says Dave, a wicked grin on his face, "but you might want to think about calling it The Montague. It would smell as sweet . . ."

The Rose

60 ml (2 oz) Noilly Prat dry vermouth
30 ml (1 oz) Trimbach kirschwasser
1 teaspoon raspberry syrup
Fill a mixing glass two-thirds full of ice and add all of the ingredients. Stir for approximately 30 seconds. Strain into a chilled cocktail glass.

A Word at the End of the Bar

I tasted The Rose cocktail for the first time at a party at 5 Ninth, the joint where Wondrich installed a fabulous cocktail menu that included this beverage, and come to think of it, that was as close as he ever came to actually buying me a drink. He wasn't actually paying, of course, but Dave was our host for the evening, so ... Run, don't walk, to try this cocktail. It's one of the best drinks I've ever had in my life.

Episode 39

The Basque Martini

The Professor, our cocktailian bartender, is very excited today—he just got a delivery of Baines Pacharán, a Spanish liqueur that's very hard to come by. Some Spanish and Basque restaurants carry this specialty product, but no liquor stores in the San Francisco area keep it in stock. They can get hold of it, though, by ordering it from the local distributor, Chrissa Imports. The Professor discovered this product when Sarah Duncan, bartender at Iluna Basque restaurant on Union Street, served him her creation, The Basque Martini, a couple of weeks ago.

Doc, one of The Professor's fervent if feisty regular customers, has been listening to The Professor rave about Pacharán ever since that night, so he, too, is happy that the product has arrived. Perhaps he can now try a Basque Martini, make the appropriate noises, and he won't have to listen to much more on the subject. Doc enjoys hanging out at the bar in the afternoon, but he prefers reading books to listening to The Professor nattering about the nuances of specialty liqueurs.

"Okay, Professor, make me a Basque Martini. Let's see what all this fuss has been about," requests Doc.

"You're gonna love this one. Promise. Did I tell you how Pacharán is made?" asks The Professor.

"Let's see. It's flavored with sloe berries, the fruit of the blackthorn bush, a member of the plum genus of the *Rosaceae*, or rose, family. It also contains a subtle hint of anise, and it's not overly sweet."

"Yes, that's right. Lots of people in Spain make homemade versions of this stuff, but the Baines family has been producing it commercially since 1959. Wait till you taste this cocktail. I've no idea how Sarah ever thought to mix Pacharán with crème de bananes, lime juice, and pineapple juice—she must think outside the box. This is one of the best new drinks I've tried in years," says The Professor, filling his cocktail shaker with ice.

"Seems I hear you say that quite often, Professor."

"Yeah, well, there are quite a few great new drinks out there these days."

The Professor has a plan to get his customers to try his new-found drink. Just before his usual after-work crowd descends on the bar he makes a couple of dozen small Basque Martinis and assembles them on a large tray on the other side of the barroom, right next to the exit sign.

Doc truly loves the Basque Martini that The Professor makes for him, and he decided to wait around to see how it's received by the 5:15-brigade. The door opens right on cue, and a group of four regulars walk through the door. The Professor points in the direction of the tray laden with ready-made cocktails and tells them to help themselves. The first to the tray, however, trips as he's approaching it, and 24 cocktails end up on the floor.

"I meant to warn you about that, Professor," says Doc.

"What?" asks The Professor, his face ashen with shock.

"You should never put all your Basques in one exit, Professor."

The Professor removes Doc's drink from that bar and bids him good-night.

The Basque Martini

Adapted from a recipe by Sarah Duncan, bartender, Iluna
Basque restaurant, San Francisco, circa 2004

45 ml (1.5 oz) Baines Pacharán

45 ml (1.5 oz) crème de bananes

60 ml (2 oz) pineapple juice

30 ml (1 oz) fresh lime juice

Fill a cocktail shaker two-thirds full of ice and add all of the
ingredients. Shake for approximately 15 seconds. Strain into
a chilled cocktail glass.

A Word at the End of the Bar

This is indeed a counter-intuitive drink, and it's one that I've served to lots of friends and neighbors with extraordinary success. The punchline in this piece came from a certain Frank Casa, one of the owners of Drake's Drum, the Upper East Side joint where I got my first bartending gig in Manhattan in 1973. He had a shaggy-dog story about his Basque college roommate that he'd stretch out for a good long time, and it ended with "don't put all your Basques in one exit." Frank's audience would groan and walk away, and Frank would grin. Strange dude, Frank Casa. Nice guy, but strange all the same . . .

Episode 40

Applejack Rabbit

The Professor, our cocktailian bartender, is holding forth on the sweetening agents he likes to use in cocktails, and a group of bartenders from the neighborhood is seated at the bar, listening and adding comments from time to time.

"I use granulated sugar if I'm muddling citrus fruits—the sugar abrades the zests and brings out the essential oils. Otherwise I use simple syrup—one part sugar dissolved in one part water," The Professor professes.

"Ever use honey, Professor?" asks Jonathan, a visitor from England who was invited by one of the other bartenders.

"Only in Hot Toddies, and then only if it's a Toddy made with a fairly peaty scotch."

"What about maple syrup?"

"Urgh. That stuff's for pancakes and French toast only," The Professor scowls.

"Mind if I prove you wrong?" asks Jonathan.

"Be my guest, but I doubt you'll convince me."

"Okay, first let's look at which bottlings of calvados you have behind the bar, and while we're doing that, perhaps someone can get me some maple syrup from the kitchen. Make sure it's the real stuff, though," Jonathan admonishes.

Regina, the somewhat raunchy waitress, heads off toward the kitchen while The Professor starts pulling bottles of calvados from the backbar and placing them in front of Jonathan. Calvados is a French apple brandy that must be made in the Calvados region of Normandy. The finest bottlings, designated as Calvados du Pays d'Auge, are distilled in pot stills, like cognacs, and bear flavorful apple notes that lie under an austere blanket of dry spiciness. Recommendable brands of calvados include Busnel, Boulard, Camut, Coeur de Lion, Daron, and Père Magloire. Distinctive American apple brandies such as Laird's 12-year-old Rare Apple Brandy, and the Eau de Vie de Pomme made at the Clear Creek Distillery in Oregon, are also well worth seeking.

With The Professor's permission, Jonathan steps behind the bar and proceeds to prepare the cocktail. "I learned this one from Julien Gualdoni, head bartender at a cocktail bar in London called The Player—this guy really knows his stuff," he tells the assembled mass. "Until I tasted the Applejack Rabbit I was of the same mind as The Professor—maple syrup was for breakfast only."

The drink gets passed down the bar. Everyone, including The Professor, takes a sip.

"Okay," says The Professor, "I concede. Maple syrup ain't just for breakfast anymore." The other bartenders concur—this is a spectacular drink.

"Personally, I've never restricted the use of maple syrup to breakfast," says Regina.

"You've used it in mixed drinks before?" The Professor enquires.

"That's not what I said," Regina grins. "Maple syrup can also make a good nightcap. Providing it's drizzled on the right person, of course ..."

The Applejack Rabbit

Adapted from a recipe by Julien Gualdoni, Head Bartender, The Player, London.

90 ml (3 oz) calvados

60 ml (2 oz) pure maple syrup

45 ml (1.5 oz) fresh orange juice

45 ml (1.5 oz) fresh lemon juice

Cinnamon sugar

Fill a cocktail shaker two-thirds full of ice and add all of the ingredients. Shake for approximately 15 seconds. Strain into a chilled cocktail glass rimmed with cinnamon sugar.

A Word at the End of the Bar

The Jonathan in this tale is Jonathan Downey, the guy who heads up the worldwide Match Bar empire of cocktail bars, and a man who made me feel very welcome when I first visited him at The Player, one of his London joints. I tasted the Applejack Rabbit that night, and a gang of us went on to have drinkies at Milk and Honey, another one of Jonathan's London bars, finishing up with some grand Italian food in Soho. It was a night to remember, as is every night when you make a new friend.

Episode 41

The Goldfish Cocktail

"I think you've gotten your dates mixed up. I'm quite sure that students were swallowing live fish of some kind or other in the 1920s."

"No. It was sometime at the end of the thirties. I'm positive..."

The two strangers at The Professor's bar keep arguing, but our cocktailian bartender decides to ignore them. He wanders down to see how Doc, a longtime regular, is doing. As is his wont, Doc is spending the afternoon poring over a newly acquired book.

Doc looks up from his book: "I think I'd like to try a Goldfish Cocktail, please, Professor."

"What's with all the fish today?" asks The Professor. "And I've never heard of a Goldfish Cocktail—where did you dig this one up?"

"It's detailed in this fascinating book, *On the Town in New York* by Michael and Ariane Batterberry. Apparently the drink was featured at the Aquarium speakeasy during Prohibition. Here, take a look..."

The Professor reads the pertinent passage in the book and pauses to think about the recipe—it calls for equal parts gin, dry vermouth, and Danziger Goldwasser.

Danziger Goldwasser, made by the German company Der Lachs, is an herbal liqueur that dates back to the late 1500s. It's flavored with a blend of spices and other botanicals, and although we know that caraway and orange zest are among the ingredients, the complete recipe is a company secret. Flecks of 22-karat gold are suspended in this liqueur, but don't worry, the gold won't harm your system. Alchemists who ceaselessly sought to create the water of life used pure gold in many concoctions—it's doubtful, though, that ingesting it will prolong your days on earth. Goldschlager, a high-proof cinnamon-flavored schnapps, is the other popular liqueur that contains flecks of real gold, but gold is the only thing that these two products have in common.

"I'll make the drink, but I'm going to alter the ratios a little—Goldwasser could dominate the drink at these proportions."

The Professor assembles his version of a Goldfish Cocktail and presents it to Doc. With a little imagination the gold flakes floating in the glass could bring goldfish to mind, but the complexity of the drink itself is what's really startling.

"This is a real winner, Professor," exclaims Doc. "Allow me to buy two of these fine drinks for our new friends down the bar, and give them these notes, in this order, would you?" Doc folds two pieces of paper on which he's been scribbling for the past few minutes. He hands them to The Professor.

Our bartender makes two more drinks, places them in front of the strangers, along with the first note from Doc, and tells them who has paid for the cocktails. They raise their glasses towards Doc, take a sip of their cocktails, and the taller of the two men unfolds the paper.

"What's it say?" asks the second guy.

"On a ten-dollar bet, Lothrop Withington, Jr. swallowed a live goldfish at Harvard on March 3, 1939," the tall man reads. "Ah, what does he know? Swallowing live fish was a Roaring Twenties' fad."

The Professor hands him the second note. It contains a Mark Twain quote: "Don't tell fish stories where the people know you; but particularly, don't tell them where they know the fish."

The Goldfish Cocktail

A Prohibition-era drink. This formula was adapted from a drink detailed in *On the Town in New York* by Michael and Ariane Batterberry.

60 ml (2 oz) gin

30 ml (1 oz) dry vermouth

15 ml (.5 oz) Danziger Goldwasser

Fill a mixing glass two-thirds full of ice and add all of the ingredients. Stir for approximately 30 seconds. Strain into a chilled cocktail glass.

A Word at the End of the Bar

Michael and Ariane Batterberry founded *Food & Wine* magazine and *Food Arts* magazine, and it was Michael who gave me my first ever magazine assignment in 1990. I owe a lot to Michael Batterberry. Thanks Michael, you're a class act.

Episode 42

Corpse Reviver No. 2

Hal, a regular at The Professor's bar, isn't feeling great today—he had just a couple of drinks more than he should have last night, and there's a tiny gnome in his head pushing on the back of his eyeballs with its thumbs while at the same time its feet are beating a mambo rhythm on the back of poor Hal's skull.

"Would it be possible to get a large cup of coffee and perhaps a hunk of the hair of the dog?" he asks our cocktailian bartender.

"The hair of the dog that bit you is only going to delay the inevitable, Hal. But if you insist, perhaps you'd like to try a Corpse Reviver?" The Professor suggests.

"Whatever you say, Professor. Whatever you say."

The Corpse Reviver is detailed in William Grimes' book, *Straight Up or On The Rocks*, as a drink that was available at the

1867 Parisian Exposition Universelle. Over 60 years later the cocktail had crossed the English Channel and had evolved into two different recipes—No. 1 and No. 2—both of which were served at the Savoy Hotel in London.

Harry Craddock, the bartender who compiled *The Savoy Cocktail Book*, published in 1930, noted that Corpse Reviver No. 1 should be "taken before 11 a.m., or whenever steam and energy are needed." And following the No. 2 recipe he advised that, "Four of these taken in swift succession will unrevive the corpse again." The only things the two recipes have in common is that both are fairly high in alcohol and both contain wines that have been infused with many different botanicals and fortified with a little brandy.

The aromatized wine in the Corpse Reviver No. 1 is sweet vermouth, whereas the second recipe calls for Lillet Blanc, an apéritif wine that, in a literal sense, could be called a vermouth. The same could be said about Dubonnet Blanc, but both of these products are a little sweeter and fruitier than most dry vermouths and bear heavier bodies.

"Here's a Corpse Reviver No. 2, Hal. Sip it slowly."

A young woman enters the bar. She walks over to Hal and asks how he's feeling.

"Professor, one more Corpse Reviver, please. Christine here joined me at a couple of bars last night, and she probably needs one as much as I do."

The Professor makes a second cocktail, sets it down on the bar in front of Christine, and offers a little Irish toast in sympathy: "May the road rise up to meet you."

"Would that it had done that last night," says Christine. "Unfortunately Hal and I decided to stumble on our way home. We met the road at its own level."

Corpse Reviver No. 2

22.5 ml (.75 oz) dry gin
22.5 ml (.75 oz) Cointreau
22.5 ml (.75 oz) Lillet Blanc or Dubonnet Blanc
22.5 ml (.75 oz) fresh lemon juice
1 dash Pernod
Fill a cocktail shaker two-thirds full of ice and add all of the ingredients. Shake for approximately 15 seconds. Strain into a chilled cocktail glass.

A Word at the End of the Bar

The Hal in this story is a certain Chris Hallerton, and although he isn't tending bar at the time of this writing, he remains one of my very favorite bartenders of all time. Chris used to hold forth from behind the mahogany at Duffy's, a very solid Irish joint in Hoboken. He attended one of my Cocktails in the Country classes, circa 2004, and one night he and Christine—whose last name I can't for the life of me remember but I think she worked at a tiki joint in Brooklyn—did indeed tie one on in a very serious manner, so I used them in this piece to give them a little documentation, as it were.

Chris—whose nickname is Hal but doesn't let just anyone use it—is now a very happily married man, and his wife, the luverly Ann, gave birth to John "Jack" Geoffrey Hallerton, a boy who "came roaring into the world April 8, 2008 at 11:20 a.m."

Episode 43

Julia's Cup

The Professor is taking a break this week so that I can take a little time to remember Julia Child, perhaps America's best-loved chef, who died last Friday, two days shy of her 92nd birthday. I never met Ms. Child, though we were once in the same room and her presence was palpable. I did, however, talk with her on the telephone twice and came close to feeling her wrath on one of those occasions.

In the early 1990s, when I was just starting to write professionally, I was asked to pen a piece on vermouth for a trade magazine. "Call Julia Child," I was told. "She swigged vermouth from the bottle on television once."

"I most certainly did not." Ms. Child informed me. There was an edge to her voice. "And I'm happy to report that the man who started that rumor isn't doing very well professionally," she added. I detected a little triumph. Julia did admit to enjoying vermouth, though, and she was known to favor it over white wine when cooking. Her first book, *Mastering the Art of French Cooking*, written with Louisette Bertholle and Simone Beck, advises that, "a good, dry, white vermouth is an excellent substitute, and much better than the wrong kind of white wine."

My second conversation with Julia occurred about eight years ago when I was seeking quotes from celebrities about Martinis. Her assistant answered the phone, but it wasn't long before I had Julia's ear. She told me about her first Martinis, prepared by a college friend's two uncles who lived close to the campus. She confessed, though, that she no longer had the tolerance for a drink as strong as the Dry Gin Martini. She did, however, indulge in Reverse Martinis, a glass full of dry vermouth on the rocks—she preferred Noilly Prat—topped off with a small floater of gin: "I really like Gordon's gin, and it's not too expensive." Julia boasted that she could polish off two Martinis made in this fashion.

Julia Child's family requested that a moment of silence be observed in her honor last Saturday night at 8 o'clock, feeling that it was appropriate she be remembered during dinner. And Ted and Linda Fondulas, owners of Hemingway's Restaurant in Killington, Vermont, where for a ten-year period Ms. Child occasionally celebrated, named a specialty cocktail in Julia's honor.

"Julia loved chefs and restaurants. She realized how difficult the profession [is] so she was always supportive of the business. She went out of her way to say hello to the kitchen staff and pose for photo ops, always asking about them, wanting to hear about their lives. She was generous with her time and knowledge—in short a wonderful person of which the world will have one less," said Linda Fondulas.

Julia's Cup contains a brandy base and green Chartreuse, a French herbal liqueur, said to have been created by Carthusian monks in 1737. I'm sure Julia would approve of that combination. As for the base of the drink, if *Mastering the Art of French Cooking* is anything to go by, Julia would make sure that the brandy was cognac: "Because there are dreadful concoctions bottled under the label of brandy, we have specified cognac whenever brandy is required," the book instructs. Since it's too late to observe last Saturday's moment of silence, I'm going to suggest a small ritual be attached to this drink. When the cocktails are made, raise your glasses, and move as if to clink them together, but don't allow your glasses to touch. This will be the silence in Julia's honor.

Wherever you are, Julia, know that we'll always remember you with love, and whatever you do up there remember not to swig from that vermouth bottle. At least not while the Big Guy's watching.

Julia's Cup

Adapted from a recipe created at Hemingway's Restaurant, Killington, Vermont.

30 ml (1 oz) cognac

7.5 ml (.25 oz) green Chartreuse

1 teaspoon simple syrup

1 teaspoon fresh lemon juice

Champagne

Fill a cocktail shaker two-thirds full of ice and add the cognac, Chartreuse, simple syrup, and lemon juice. Shake for approximately 15 seconds. Strain into a chilled cocktail glass. Top with the champagne.

A Word at the End of the Bar

've nothing to add to this one. It speaks for itself, I think. I'm so happy that I spoke to Julia Child a couple of times, though—her magic could be felt even on the other end of a phone call.

Episode 44

The Algonquin Cocktail

t's lunch time, and Ken, a regular at The Professor's bar, steps up to the mahogany. His clothes are soaking wet.

"I just got caught in an incredible downpour, and now the sun's shining again. Just my luck."

"You'd better get out of those wet clothes and into a Dry Martini," The Professor quips.

"The world just loves a smarty-pants bartender, Professor. Who said that anyway? Robert Benchley?"

"Nobody really knows, Ken, but it's been attributed to him. Probably one of the Algonquin Round Table bunch—if not Benchley it could have been Dorothy Parker, Noel Coward, or even Harpo Marx. How about an Algonquin Cocktail to mark the occasion?"

"Depends on which rye whiskeys you have back there," Ken tells The Professor.

New York's literati set gathered around the Algonquin Round Table, trading quips, picking on celebrities, and generally keeping each other entertained for the whole of the 1920s. The Algonquin Cocktail didn't originate at that time, though—it's a more recent creation calling for straight rye whiskey, a spirit that's misunderstood by many people.

Blended whisky, from Canada and the U.S., is often erroneously known as rye whiskey. This is because during Prohibition—1920 to 1933—massive quantities of blended Canadian whisky were smuggled into the States and sold as rye. True rye whiskey, made with at least 51 percent rye grain, is a different product entirely—it's often spicy and almost perfumy in nature, whereas blended whisky tends to be sweeter and far more fruity on the palate.

"We have Old Overholt straight rye, Rittenhouse, Van Winkle Family Reserve 13-year-old, Wild Turkey, and I think I still have a little of the Sazerac 18-year-old left."

"Well, I usually go for the Wild Turkey—it's a great straightforward rye—but I'm soaked to the skin so I think I deserve something special. Make it with the Sazerac, please."

As The Professor makes Ken's drink, Regina, the raunchy waitress who's taking a day off from work and embarking on a pub crawl, strolls into the bar.

"This is my first stop, Professor. I'll try whatever Ken's drinking."

Ken and Regina chat about which other bars she's going to visit, and after fixing Regina's cocktail The Professor disappears down the bar to take care of some other customers. Soon, though, he's back: "Regina, Doc would like to buy you a drink, and Mark wants to send you one, too."

"Oooh, this has all the makings of a great afternoon. Set 'em up, Professor. Ken, will you excuse me while I go say hi to the guys?" Regina sashays down the bar.

The Professor shakes his head. "That woman speaks eighteen languages and can't say 'no' in any of them," he tells Ken.

"Your line, Professor?"

"No, it was one of Dorothy Parker's lines, I'm afraid."

The Algonquin Cocktail

45 ml (1.5 oz) straight rye whiskey

22.5 ml (.75 oz) dry vermouth

22.5 ml (.75 oz) pineapple juice

Fill a cocktail shaker two-thirds full of ice and add all of the ingredients. Shake for approximately 15 seconds. Strain into a chilled cocktail glass.

A Word at the End of the Bar

I'm writing this in 2010, and there's a whole bunch of young bartenders out there who have no idea how tough it used to be to get straight rye in a bar, just five or six years ago. Thank God that's no longer true. Paul Pacult and I played a small role in getting the Van Winkle bottlings on the shelves, by the way. We bumped into Julian Van Winkle at the Kentucky Bourbon Festival one year, and he told us that he was going to issue some straight ryes, but only in Japan. We beat mercilessly him until he changed his mind . . .

Episode 45

Hoskins Cocktail

John and Fiona Hoskins, an English couple on vacation from the green and pleasant land, have just taken stools at The Professor's bar. Our cocktailian bartender walks over to greet them.

"Good afternoon, folks. You look like you're ready for a drink."

"We certainly are," John agrees, "it's a little too hot out there for our liking. First, though, we're supposed to tell you that Chuck Taggart and Wesly Moore from Pasadena say hi."

"Ah, you know the Gumbo Guys, huh? What have they been up to lately?"

John and Fiona tell The Professor that their mutual friends—Chuck hosts a blog called Gumbo Pages, hence the nickname—have been busy creating new drinks, as is their wont, and they've brought The Professor the recipe for the Hoskins Cocktail, a drink Chuck formulated specifically for John and Fiona.

"Let's have a look at this drink," says The Professor. He studies the ingredients. "So, Chuck's using Torani Amer, huh? This is going to be interesting." The Professor wanders down the bar to show the piece of paper to a couple of off-duty bartenders who have popped in to pass a little time on their day off.

Torani Amer is a liqueur made in a similar style to Amer Picon, a French apéritif with notes of bitter oranges, cinchona bark, and gentian. It's almost impossible to find Amer Picon in the States these days, but people who knew the product when it was available swear that the Torani product tastes very much like the original. It is a very sophisticated liqueur, and probably not to everyone's taste, but people who enjoy Italian bitters such as Fratelli Averna will likely love Torani Amer, and some folk who usually shun such products might just enjoy it in the Hoskins Cocktail.

John and Fiona watch as The Professor assembles the Hoskins Cocktail, carefully flaming a twist of orange peel on top of the drink just as the instructions require. Our bartender takes a sip, closes his eyes, and mulls. His eyes open. They're sparkling.

"Guys, just try this. It's nothing short of a masterpiece." He offers the glass to the off-duty bartenders who each taste the drink, and agree heartily with The Professor.

"Did you taste the oranges in the Cointreau marrying beautifully with the oranges in the Amer? And how about that maraschino liqueur? There's just a touch in there, but that beautiful nuttiness just shines through the bitter botanicals and makes itself known. And the gin! The Plymouth—it's perfect in this drink."

He walks back down the bar to John and Fiona.

"You guys must be ecstatic. This is an incredible cocktail, and Chuck named it for you. What do you think? Isn't it great?"

"You must listen carefully if you want to know what I truly think, Professor." Fiona leans over the mahogany to get closer to our bartender. The Professor is somewhat taken aback, but he leans in so his guest can speak directly into his ear. "I think, Professor, that this location would be a fine place to open a bar. Do you think it's possible that we could get a couple of beers before we bloody well die of thirst in here?"

The Hoskins Cocktail

Adapted from a recipe by Chuck Taggart, circa 2004.

60 ml (2 oz) Plymouth gin

22.5 ml (.75 oz) Torani Amer

15 ml (.5 oz) maraschino liqueur

7.5 ml (.25 oz) Cointreau

1 dash orange bitters

1 orange twist, as garnish

Fill a mixing glass two-thirds full of ice and add all of the ingredients. Stir for a minimum of 30 seconds. Strain into a chilled cocktail glass. Light a match and hold it close to the top of the drink. Take the orange twist in your other hand and hold it by the sides. (The colored side of the twist should be pointing toward the drink.) Now hold the twist over the match and squeeze it to release its oils. You will see them sparkle as they leap through the flame onto the top of the drink. Add the orange twist to the drink.

A Word at the End of the Bar

This one's pretty self-explanatory, but I know a little more about Amer Picon now, and as far as I can gather, not only is it still near-as-damn-it impossible to get outside of France, the company apparently changed their recipe in the 1970s, anyway, so if you do get a bottle, it won't taste they way it did when drinks such as the Picon Punch was developed. Rumor has it that Jamie Boudreau, the famed cocktailian bartender who currently slings drinks in Seattle, has developed a recipe for a very viable substitute for Amer Picon, and if you punch the following string into your browser you can go look it over: http://spiritsandcocktails.wordpress.com/2007/09/09/amer-picon/

The Thoroughbred Cocktail

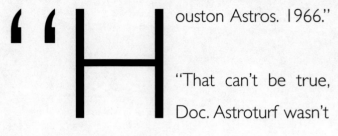

"**H**ouston Astros. 1966."

"That can't be true, Doc. Astroturf wasn't patented until 1967," says The Professor, our cocktailian bartender.

"I'm telling you the Houston Astros were the first ball team to play on Astroturf, and they played on it in 1966. The stuff was actually named for the AstroDome. It was called Chemturf when they first came up with it."

Doc and The Professor are both correct. Although Astroturf, developed as a way to provide urban dwellers with surfaces on which to exercise, didn't receive a patent until July 25, 1967, the Houston Astros first played on Astroturf in a game against the L. A. Dodgers on April 8, 1966.

"Astroturf? I just put Astroturf down in my office so I can practice my putting." The Boss, who has been eavesdropping for the last few minutes, decides to join in the discussion. "Wait here, I'll bring a piece up from the basement. It's fascinating stuff."

The Professor rolls his eyes at Doc, and strolls down the bar to serve Dean and Mike, a couple of bartenders on one of their frequent visits to San Francisco from their native Canada.

"Any new cocktails for us to try, Professor?" asks Dean.

"Actually I just got a recipe from Nick Burns. He works at the Arterra restaurant at the San Diego Marriott near the Del Mar racetrack. Wanna try it?"

"Del Mar, huh? Didn't Bing Crosby used to croon a song about that track?" asks Mike.

"Don't know, Mike. Wanna try this drink or not? It's called The Thoroughbred."

"Sure. Let's give it a spin."

The Thoroughbred Martini is made with Hangar 1 Mandarin Blossom vodka, an intensely flavored product made by Jorg Rupf of St. George Spirits in a former WWII structure—Hangar 1—at the Alameda Naval Air Station. Rupf also produces Buddha's Hand Citron vodka, Kaffir Lime vodka, and a newly released Fraser River Raspberry vodka that will be issued seasonally in small quantities. The flavored vodkas from Hangar 1 have been widely heralded by more than a couple of spirits experts—they are wonderful hand-crafted products made by craftsmen, not technicians.

The Professor sets down a pair of Thoroughbred Martinis on the bar in front of Dean and Mike. The drinks are pale blue in color due to a dash of blue curaçao in the recipe.

"Good gosh, Professor, this is as blue as the Pacific Ocean," says Dean. He takes a sip. "Tastes beautiful, too," he adds.

The Boss appears at the bar and slaps down a piece of his new office carpeting on the bar, knocking Mike's drink all over the synthetic grass before he even has a chance to get the glass to his mouth.

"Ooops. Sorry. Just a little excited about my new putting green," he offers.

"That's okay," says Mike. "Professor—I've remembered the name of that song that Crosby used to sing about the Del Mar Racetrack."

"What is it, Mike?"

"'Where the Surf Meets the Turf,' Professor. 'Where the Surf Meets the Turf.'"

The Thoroughbred Martini

Adapted from a recipe by Nick Burns, Arterra restaurant at the San Diego Marriott, circa 2004.

60 ml (2 oz) Hangar 1 Mandarin Blossom vodka

30 ml (1 oz) Cointreau

1 splash blue curaçao

1 splash fresh grapefruit juice

1 orange twist, as garnish

Fill a cocktail shaker two-thirds full of ice and add all of the ingredients. Shake for approximately 15 seconds. Strain into a chilled cocktail glass. Add the garnish.

A Word at the End of the Bar

Dean and Mike are a couple of flair bartenders from Canada who attended one of my Cocktails in the Country workshops a few years ago, and they wowed the regulars at Painter's, where the classes were held, with a pretty astonishing display of their very own brand of magic. You can find these guys at Flairco.com, and Dean is also involved with a Kentucky-based operation known as The Finest Call.

Episode 47

V Sting

"**A**daptation. Now there's a great movie for you," says, Paul, a new customer at The Professor's bar who thinks of himself as an aficionado of the silver screen. He's a nice enough guy, but he can drone on a little. "And the director, that Spike Jonze guy, is the same guy who directed **Being John Malkovich**. There's another sterling flick. Same screenwriter, too. Charlie Kaufman."

The Professor admits to having seen neither of these movies, but since it's a quiet afternoon he asks about the plot lines. Our cocktailian bartender likes to cultivate new customers, even the boring ones.

"The John Malkovich flick was real weird, man. All these people got to live inside the Malkovich's head by going through this portal, see, and, well, er, you've kinda got to see it."

"And **Adaptation**?" The Professor asks.

"*Adaptation* was way cool. It's about this screenwriter who's trying to write a movie based on Susan Orlean's book *The Orchid Thief*. He gets writer's block, though, and, er, well, you've kind of got to see it," Paul admits.

"Orchids. There's something I know about. Just one kind of orchid, though. Vanilla," The Professor tells Paul.

"Vanilla's an orchid?"

"From what I've been told it's the only edible fruit of the orchid family. I know more about vanilla-flavored spirits and liqueurs, though. They seem to be really hot right now."

The Professor is right. There are many vanilla vodkas on the shelves from companies such as Absolut, Grey Goose, Skyy, Stoli, and Van Gogh; vanilla-flavored rums from Bacardi, Mount Gay, and Whaler's are also catching on with cocktail connoisseurs, and the company that makes Grand Marnier has just issued Navan, an incredibly wonderful new liqueur with a cognac base that's flavored with Madagascar vanilla. Rather than being overly sweet, as some liqueurs are wont to be, Navan is on the dry side. It's an austere, sophisticated product.

"So, Professor, you have any drinks made with vanilla? I fancy sipping an orchid in tribute to *Adaptation*."

"Yep, I just got a recipe from Albert Trummer—the guy on the East Coast who calls himself a bar chef. The original recipe's pretty simple so I like to add a couple of dashes of bitters to it to spice it up a little. Want one?"

"Sure thing, Professor. Bring it on. You're my man."

The Professor turns his back, rolls his eyes at Doc, his friend sitting at the other end of the bar, and assembles a V-Sting. The drink is made with Navan and either Hennessy Paradis Extra

or Hennessy VSOP Privilège cognac. Hennessy Paradis is a tad expensive at around $250 per bottle, but the Privilège bottling is fairly affordable at about $40. He dashes some bitters on top of the drink, stirs it, and offers it to Paul.

"So Professor, if this isn't the original recipe, it's sort of an adaptation, isn't it?"

"I guess so, Paul."

"Pretty cool, Professor. I'm sipping an orchid adaptation and toasting *Adaptation*, a movie about orchids."

"Just drink it, would you, Paul?" The Professor walks down the bar to chat with Doc. Sometimes enough is enough.

V Sting

Adapted from a recipe by Albert Trummer, Bar Chef at Trummer Home, Greenpoint, New York.

60 ml (2 oz) Navan

60 ml (2 oz) Hennessy Paradis Extra or Hennessy VSOP Privilège cognac

2 dashes Angostura bitters (optional)

1 orange slice, as garnish

1 vanilla bean, as garnish

Fill a large old-fashioned glass with ice and add the Navan, cognac, and bitters (if using). Stir briefly. Add the garnishes.

A Word at the End of the Bar

I met Albert Trummer only once that I can recall. It was at a party for Dave Wondrich's book, *Esquire Drinks,* in 2004, and Albert won a competition held that night by making one of the very best Dry Gin Martinis I've ever had. I had a problem at the time with the term "bar chef," so I tackled Albert about it, and he admirably explained that he had spent years in Europe training to be a bartender and learning to make all his own syrups and myriad other ingredients, so I let him off the hook. He's a nice guy.

Episode 48

The Spanish Rose

The Professor is polishing the liquor bottles behind the bar and humming a tune that Doc, the most regular regular at the other side of our cocktailian bartender's slab of mahogany, doesn't recognize.

"I can't name that tune no matter how many notes you hum, Professor. Of course, you being completely out of tune doesn't make it any easier."

"Being tone deaf is an advantage in life, Doc. For me everyone's in tune all the time. Nobody ever goes flat or sharp, and every singer hits every note. It's a very harmonious world I live in."

"Yes, very nice, Professor, but what tune is that supposed to be?"

"'Spanish Rose', Doc. 'Spanish Rose.'"

Doc takes issue with this and tells The Professor that no matter how badly he's out of tune, the song he's humming is not "Spanish Rose." He sings a few lines of the song for The Professor.

"That isn't 'Spanish Rose,' Doc."

"It most certainly is. It's from **Bye Bye Birdie**, the musical satire that opened on Broadway in 1960."

"That explains a lot, Doc. My 'Spanish Rose' is a song by Van Morrison. Just a little more hip than your version I think . . . . Let's not argue about it, though. Let's drink a Spanish Rose instead. My shift ends in half an hour and I'm having a night on the town. Nothing like getting a head start."

Bar Manager David Nepove created the drink known as the Spanish Rose at Enrico's restaurant, on Broadway at Kearny, using Licor 43, as its sweetening agent. Licor 43 is a Spanish liqueur flavored with 43 different herbs, spices, and fruits, and bears fragrant vanilla and orange notes. It isn't used too often by cocktailian bartenders, but herbal liqueurs can bring much diversity to mixed drinks.

Galliano, another herbal liqueur, won both gold and silver medals in San Francisco's International Wine and Spirits Competition earlier this year, and this bottling brings faint anise notes into the picture, too. It marries very well to smoky scotches.

The Professor makes two of Nepove's drinks and places one at each side of Doc. He stands back, takes the bar's digital camera from a drawer and asks Doc to smile. The Professor snaps a shot and thanks Doc for posing.

"What was that all about, Professor?

"Just wanted a shot of a thorn between two roses, Doc. I'm about to leave the bar now. Care to bar-hop with me for a while?"

The Spanish Rose

Adapted from a recipe by David Nepove, Bar Manager, Enrico's, San Francisco.

1 rosemary sprig

22.5 ml (.75 oz) fresh lemon juice

45 ml (1.5 oz) Plymouth gin

22.5 ml (.75 oz) Licor 43

15 ml (.5 oz) cranberry juice

Strip the leaves from the bottom half of the rosemary sprig and place in them in a mixing glass. Add the lemon juice and muddle well. Add ice, the gin, and the Licor 43; shake for approximately 15 seconds. Strain into an ice-filled wine goblet, place the remaining rosemary stem in the glass. Top with the cranberry juice.

A Word at the End of the Bar

David Nepove is one of my favorite bartenders in San Francisco, and I actually got to know him a little better when we were both invited on a tour of tequila distilleries with the infamous Julio Bermejo in 2005. David, in case you've never met him, is a tall guy, and by the looks of his biceps he works out like a fiend, too, but he's a very gentle giant. Nevertheless I told him in no uncertain terms that if he should start any trouble in Mexico, I'd be the one to take him down. He patted the top of my head and smiled.

The Secret Cocktail

The Professor, our cocktailian bartender, is having a problem with a customer who doesn't seem to know what she wants to drink.

"How can I make you a cocktail if you won't tell me which cocktail you want?"

"It's a secret cocktail."

"Can you tell me the ingredients?"

"Yes, but it's still a secret."

"Your name isn't Abbott or Costello by any chance?"

The woman holds out her hand. "Nope. Janet's the name. Ted Haigh told me to say hi."

"Ah, you're a friend of Dr. Cocktail. I haven't seen him in a while. He ever finish that book?"

"Where d'ya think I found the recipe for the Secret Cocktail?"

Vintage Spirits & Forgotten Cocktails, a new book by Ted Haigh, has just been released by Rockport Publishers. In addition to detailing recipes for 80 superb cocktails that were in danger of being lost to history, Haigh also describes and gives sources for such obscure liqueurs and spirits as Parfait Amour, which he portrayed as tasting like a "delicate combination of grape jelly beans and marshmallows," that's made by the Marie Brizard brand. He also zeroes in on Swedish Punsch, a Scandinavian rum-based liqueur available on the Internet (www.northerner.com) that's a must if you want to make a true Have a Heart Cocktail.

Janet tells The Professor how to make the Secret Cocktail and while he fixes it for her he wonders out loud, "I'm pretty sure I use to make this drink back in the seventies, but I can't for the life of me remember what we used to call it.,"

"Yep. Ted says it was popular back then, but he doesn't think many people would order it today under its original name."

"Why's that?"

"Just a bit sappy sounding. The drink's great, though."

The Professor strains the Secret Cocktail into a chilled cocktail glass. When he sees the color of the drink a light goes off in his head.

"I got it! I know what this drink is. It's a . . . Nope. Dr. Cocktail's right. We'll just keep calling it the Secret Cocktail and leave it at that."

The Boss walks into the bar and stops in his tracks when he sees the Secret Cocktail on the bar. "My God! Is that . . ."

The Professor is quick on his feet and jumps in before the Boss can utter the original name of the drink. "Boss. Shut up this instant. You'll jinx the drink."

"What? What's the story?"

"It's a secret, Boss. Just leave it at that, wouldja?"

The Boss shakes his head and disappears to his office. The Professor waits until he hears the office door close and turns back to his new friend. "Wanna know another secret?"

"What's that, Professor?"

"The Boss still believes he's the boss."

The Secret Cocktail

Adapted from a recipe in *Vintage Spirits & Forgotten Cocktails* by Ted Haigh, a.k.a. Dr. Cocktail.

45 ml (1.5 oz) gin

15 ml (.5 oz) applejack

15 ml (.5 oz) fresh lemon juice

1 egg white (see note)

2 dashes grenadine

1 maraschino cherry, as garnish

Fill a cocktail shaker two-thirds full of ice and add the gin, applejack, lemon juice, egg white, and grenadine. Shake for approximately 15 seconds. Strain into a chilled cocktail glass. Add the garnish.

Note: According to some studies, uncooked eggs may not be safe because in rare instances they may carry salmonella.

A Word at the End of the Bar

read the whole of Doc Cocktail's's book in one sitting, and if you don't have a copy I heartily recommend that you rush out and get one, right now. You'll find out the true name of the Secret Cocktail, too ... Lest you're wondering, I can no longer find Swedish Punsch on that Northerner web site, but a good search engine yielded three sources for it very quickly, so if you'd like a Have a Heart cocktail, you're going to have to surf before you make it.

Episode 50

The Monkey Gland Cocktail

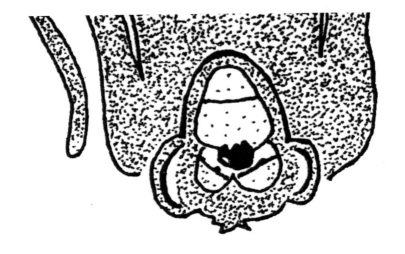

The Professor, our cocktailian bartender, is real busy. He's working a Friday night shift for a bartender who's on vacation, and he got only a one-hour break after his regular day shift. He grabbed a bite to eat and downed a swift Martini in an attempt to jump-start himself into action. Now it's almost midnight and his body's telling him he should take another break. No chance, though. The bar's six-deep with weekend revelers.

"Two G and Ts, a glass of Chablis, and a Monkey Gland Cocktail, Professor," Regina, the raunchy waitress, yells from the service end of the bar.

"English or American?" The Professor asks.

"True blue daughter of my Uncle Sam," Regina grins.

"Not you. The Monkey Gland. Ask your customer."

Regina darts off to a table where two couples are waiting for drinks and starts to interrogate the guy who ordered the questionable cocktail

The Monkey Gland Cocktail was detailed in , 1930, compiled by Harry Craddock, an American bartender who plied his trade at London's Savoy Hotel while the U.S.A endured Prohibition. The recipe calls for absinthe, an anise-flavored spirit that gained notoriety in the early twentieth century and was thought to cause insanity and a host of other maladies among its devotees, though it's quite possible that absinthe was dangerous merely because of its high alcohol content.. Absinthe has been illegal here since 1912, and sweeter substitutes, notably Absente, Herbsaint, or Pernod, are used in recipes calling for this spirit.

New York bartender Patrick Gavin Duffy introduced the Monkey Gland to America in a 1934 book, *The Official Mixer's Manual.*, Duffy inexplicably chose Bénédictine, a honeyed herbal liqueur said to have been developed in 1510 by the Bénédictine monk Dom Bernardo Vincelli, to use as an accent in the drink instead of absinthe. As a result, two versions of the cocktail, both with merit but very different from each other, are recognized as being authentic. Thus the English Monkey Gland takes an absinthe substitute, and the American version calls for Bénédictine.

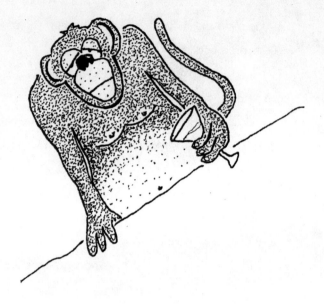

The interesting thing about these two drinks is that people who don't enjoy anise don't seem to mind it at all when it's served in a Monkey Gland, and the Bénédictine version of the cocktail is enjoyed by folk who don't usually get pleasure from herbal liqueurs. It can be fun to play around with drinks like this one, trying other liqueurs instead of either of the traditional accents.

Regina returns to the bar. "He says the English version is the only one worthy of a cocktail glass, Professor."

"He's entitled to be wrong. Duffy's version is a great drink. Which do you prefer, Regina?"

"English, American, makes no never mind to me."

The Professor eyes the waitress sternly.

"I'm talking cocktails, Regina."

"Me too, Professor. Me too." Regina flips The Professor a wink and leaves our bartender slapping his forehead.

The Monkey Gland Cocktail

60 ml (2 oz) gin
30 ml (1 oz) fresh orange juice
1 splash Bénédictine or 1 splash Pernod
1 splash grenadine
Fill a cocktail shaker two-thirds full of ice and add all of the ingredients. Shake for approximately 15 seconds and strain into a chilled cocktail glass.

A Word at the End of the Bar

I always made my Monkey Glands with Bénédictine, and it wasn't until I saw Dale DeGroff whip one up at The Rainbow Room that I knew about the English version. "What the hell are you doing?" I asked Dale. And Dale, of course, in his usual affable manner, put me straight on the matter. I still think that both versions are viable, and now that we can, once again, get real absinthe, that's what I use to make my English-style Monkey Glands.

Lest you're not sure where the term Monkey Gland came from, it's all about Dr. Serge Voronoff, a guy who grafted monkey glands into men's testicles during the 1920s and '30s in France, claiming that the procedure would increase virility. Here's a nice little quote I found about this subject: "The special charm of the monkey gland treatment . . . is not something miraculous that transforms an old man into a boy; it leaves one an old man in every important respect while giving one back one's youthful energy. Hence its appeal to the old. It has apparently every possible advantage except that it kills you." *The Freeman*, Volume 3, by Francis Neilson, Albert Jay Nock, 1921.

Episode 51

The Kew Club

The Professor, our cocktailian bartender, is tucking into a plate of corned beef hash and eggs at his favorite breakfast joint. Donna, the earth-mother owner of the cafe, has just placed a bowl of homemade marmalade on his table and he's debating whether or not to finish his eggs or dive right into a couple of rounds of toast slathered with the orange preserves when his peace is suddenly shattered by a group of tourists from London. The five women sit at the adjacent table and start to chatter incessantly. One of them looks over at The Professor as she peruses the menu.

"Recommend anything special here, darling?" she asks him.

"You can't go wrong with the hash or the buttermilk pancakes," he tells her, pushing his plate to one side and starting to spread the marmalade onto a slice of toast. The English woman watches him closely.

"What's that then?"

The Professor prepares another slice of toast and marmalade, places it on a napkin, and hands it to his new friend. She takes a bite and screams to her friends.

"It's a Kew Club on toast! Here, try this," she says, offering the treat to the group. Each of the women take a bite and one by one they agree. The Professor's curiosity is piqued.

"Okay, what's a Kew Club?" he asks.

"It's a drink we get at Milk and Honey, this super cocktail bar we go to in London. Pete Kendall, the head bartender there, invented it. Tastes just like this spicy marmalade."

"Recipe?"

"Hang on, darling," she says, eying her watch, "Pete should be getting into work about now, I'll ring him." Without missing a beat she pulls her cell phone out of her pocket, and within minutes she's handing The Professor a formula written on a paper napkin. The Professor pockets the recipe, thanks the group, and hands a card to one of the women as he gets up to leave.

"Come see me this afternoon. We'll try Kew Clubs at my joint."

The Kew Club calls for Orangerie, a delightful, very complex, orange-infused 10-year-old scotch whisky issued by Compass Box, a company that specializes in esoteric scotch blends. The Peat Monster is another of their offerings. It is a mingling of single malt scotches that's very smoky yet delicate. This is approachable enough to be a great introduction to the category, and sophisticated enough for connoisseurs, too.

It's five o'clock and the British women are sitting at The Professor's bar sipping Kew Clubs. They introduce themselves— Julie, Natalie, Hannah, Jackie, and Amelia—and Amelia, the woman who so rudely disturbed The Professor's morning peace , raises her glass.

"Cheers, love. You got this one down pat. Want a challenge?"

"Bring it on, Amelia."

"Well, I'm thinking that now you serve marmalade in a glass you might want to try to make other breakfast-y drinks. We'll be back here in about three months and this is what we'll be ordering." She hands The Professor a folded piece of paper.

"No peeking till we've gone." The women stand and file out of the bar. The Professor reads the note.

Corned-Beef Hash Cocktails, please. Straight-up. Pickled quail's egg garnish.

One of The Professor's regulars catches him rolling his eyes as he throws the paper into the garbage.

"Had your leg pulled again, Professor?"

Our cocktailian bartender ignores the comment and builds himself a Kew Club. It's been one of those days.

The Kew Club

Adapted from a recipe by Pete Kendall, head bartender at London's Milk and Honey club.

2 orange twists (1 as garnish)

60 ml (2 oz) Orangerie whisky

1 splash Grand Marnier

1 splash Bénédictine

3 dashes Angostura bitters

1 lemon twist, as garnish

Twist one of the orange twists into an empty old-fashioned glass and discard. Add ice, the Orangerie, Grand Marnier, Bénédictine, and bitters, and stir briefly. Light a match and hold it close to the top of the drink. Take the remaining orange twist in your other hand and hold it by the sides. (The colored side of the twist should be pointing toward the drink.) Now hold the twist over the match and squeeze it to release its oils and drop the twist into the cocktail. Repeat with the lemon twist.

A Word at the End of the Bar

If you've never tasted any of the Compass Box whiskies I suggest that you run out this instant and buy anything you can find of theirs. They issue some fabulous stuff. The women in this piece were all connected in one way or another to Jonathan Downey's Match bars in London—Milk and Honey being one of them—but Peter Kendall, who is working for Swire Hotels in Hong Kong at the time of writing, doubts that any of them are still there now. And Donna, the "earth-mother owner of the cafe" in this story, is my old friend Donna Hammond, who was head chef at Painter's, my local joint, when Mardee and I moved to the Hudson Valley in 1995. Donna got married recently, and she and her wife Anne own and run the Hudson Street Café in Cornwall-on-Hudson. I've never seen Donna look so blissful.

Episode 52

organized chaos

t's a wild afternoon at The Professor's bar. Jimi, a local photographer, is holding an exhibition of his latest work and the place is packed with the artsy set who are eager to see his new images while sipping on a cocktail or three. The Professor has his head down, not making eye contact with anyone until it's their turn to be served. It's the only way to handle a crowd like this.

A group of five people, three guys and two women, manage to jam themselves into a small space at the corner of the bar. The Professor walks over to see what they want.

"Can you turn the music down a little," one of the men asks our cocktailian bartender.

"No."

"Why not?

"Because it's at the right volume."

"You mean I have to shout like this?" The guy raises his voice a few decibels.

"You got it," says The Professor. The guy smiles large. He gets it. There's a party going on. The group orders cocktails and proceed to get in the right mood for the exhibition.

Jimi's wife, Liz, orders her third Margarita and introduces The Professor to her friend, Dan.

"What can I get for you, Dan?" The Professor asks.

"I'm not sure. Could you just make me an interesting cocktail? I don't like gin or tequila, and I'm not really a vodka drinker, either."

"Would you like a Manhattan?"

"No. Don't think so. Just make me something, please."

The Professor doesn't have time for this kind of behavior so, while Dan is chatting with Liz, his back to the bar, our bartender makes a Manhattan on the rocks, adding a splash of Elisir M. P. Roux to the glass to throw Dan off the track, and squeezing a wedge of lemon into the drink before he serves it.

Elisir M.P. Roux is a well-crafted herbal liqueur made with botanicals such as marjoram, hyssop, fennel, cinnamon, nutmeg, coriander, bitter almond, garden balsam, wild angelica, lemon peel, star anise, ginseng, and damiana. The star anise is immediately identifiable, but it's a very complex liqueur that marries well with scotch, bourbon, rye whiskey, brandy, and dark, or well aged, rums. Used judiciously, Elisir M. P. Roux adds an interesting accent to many cocktails, and it also works well in hot coffee or tea, or as an after-dinner drink when served neat, at room temperature.

Dan takes a sip of his drink. His eyes light up.

"This is wonderful, Professor. It's exactly what I wanted. How do you do that?"

The Professor has absolutely no idea what prompted him to combine those particular ingredients so he merely shrugs and wanders down the bar.

Five minutes later Dan asks The Professor for the name of the drink he's sipping, but our bartender doesn't hear him. He's too busy trying to keep up with the drinks ordered by myriad Jimi admirers.

"It's like organized chaos in this joint," he mumbles as starts to build another cocktail.

Dan turns to Liz.

"It's called organized chaos, Liz. Strange name for a drink, but if that's what The Professor calls it . . ."

organized chaos

60 ml (2 oz) Wild Turkey bourbon (101-proof)

45 ml (1.5 oz) Noilly Prat sweet vermouth

15 ml (.5 oz) Elisir M.P. Roux

1 lemon wedge, as garnish.

Fill a medium-sized wine goblet with ice, and add the bourbon, vermouth, and the Elisir M.P. Roux. Squeeze the lemon wedge into the drink and drop it into the glass. Stir briefly and serve.

A Word at the End of the Bar

I n 2004, after not setting foot behind a bar for quite some time, I got back behind the stick at Painter's, my local joint in the Hudson Valley. The guys who own this place, Sal and Pete Buttiglieri, are good friends of mine, and I'd convinced them to let me open the Gallery Bar—a smallish room that's primarily used for private parties—on Wednesday nights for an event that I called *organized chaos*. I put together a cocktail menu, set down some rules such as "don't ask us to change the volume of the music, it's at exactly the right level," and I made playlists of mostly rock and roll from the 60s and 70s with some punk thrown in for good measure, and a few hokey tunes from the fifties to make sure that people were paying attention. One minute the Sex Pistols were proclaiming that "No One is Innocent," and the next thing you'd hear might be Doris Day singing "Que Sera, Sera."

organized chaos went down well with some of the locals and I managed to scare up a bit of a following on

Wednesday nights. I made cocktail drinkers out of more than a few of them, too. I had construction workers from a site just down the street drinking Pisco Sours and Corpse Revivers, and a group of professional types—a photographer, a couple of I.T. people, a travel agent, and a few others—turned out on a regular basis to try something different from their usual glass of chardonnay or bottle of lite beer. The photographer was Jimi Ferrara, and that's who is featured in this fictional tale.

You can see Jimi's work on the cover of the first edition of *New Classic Cocktails* which features a painting of a wedge of lemon on a fork that we used to illustrate the Hennessy Martini. Funny thing is that, after we'd put the book together Jimi told us that the paining is a wedge of peach, not lemon. Jimi has also done our headshots a few times over the years—he's a fabulous photographer.

The Pear Martini

The Professor, our cocktailian bartender, is serving a dozen oysters to Pam, a regular customer at the bar, and a woman with a passion for seafood.

"Now, if you can make me a Pear Martini I'll be a very happy woman," she says.

"You got me on that one, Pam. Know how to make it?"

"Sure I do, Professor. The question was loaded. Take a look at this. Page 58." Pam hands a book to The Professor. *Cocktails in New York* by Anthony Giglio. This newly-released compilation of cocktail recipes from 100 of the Big Apple's finest restaurants and cocktail bars contains notes from Giglio on each drink and short essays on the places that serve them. The Pear Martini that Pam craves is a creation served at the Blue Ribbon restaurant on Sullivan Street, and Giglio notes that the drink got his attention because, "its sweet floral notes were perfectly balanced with acidity. The acidity is both necessary and logical with crawfish, crabs, oysters, and clams."

The Professor assembles a Pear Martini, pours it for Pam, and saves a tad in his shaker so he can taste the drink for himself.

"You couldn't spare one of those oysters, could you, Pam?" Pam pushes her plate toward The Professor and smiles as she watches our bartender slide an oyster down his throat, followed by a sip of the new cocktail.

"Yes. Yes. Perfect. Wonderful. The Belle de Brillet liqueur works real well here," The Professor gushes.

Belle de Brillet is a cognac-based liqueur infused with Williams pears grown in the Alsace region of France. Twenty two pears are needed to make one bottle of this wonderful liqueur which has been highly rated by many aficionados. It can be sipped neat as an after-dinner drink, served over ice, or as in this instance, used as a fragrant sweetening agent in a cocktail.

The bar's owner, known to everyone as simply The Boss, has been watching The Professor. He walks over to Pam.

"Mind If I try this?" he asks, and without waiting for an answer he devours an oyster from Pam's plate and takes a sip of her drink. "That's a brilliant match, Professor. Doc, come try this," The Boss shouts down the bar. Doc, a seasoned regular, strolls

down the bar, eats an oyster, and takes a sip from Pam's drink. He smiles and nods.

"John, get down here. Try this," The Boss shouts to another customer. Pam stands and quietly moves to another barstool. The Professor walks over.

"Dozen oysters and a Pear Martini, perhaps, Pam?"

"You're a mind-reader, Professor. How do you do that?"

"Just a hunch, Pam. Just a hunch."

The Pear Martini

Adapted from a recipe in *Cocktails in New York* by Anthony Giglio. Served at at the Blue Ribbon restaurant, New York, circa 2004.

60 ml (2 oz) Belle de Brillet

30 ml (1 oz) citrus vodka

30 ml (1 oz) fresh lime juice

Fill a cocktail shaker two-thirds full of ice and add all of the ingredients. Shake for approximately 15 seconds. Strain into a chilled cocktail glass.

A Word at the End of the Bar

The Pam in this tale is Pam Parshegian, the fabulous woman who edited my column in *Nation's Restaurant News* for about eleven years. That was a great gig for me, and Pam and I not only got through the whole run with no tears, I also thought of us as being a team. She edited my work flawlessly, managing to make what I'd turned in better every time, yet making the edited pieces still sound like me. Thanks Pam Parshegian. It was a privilege to work with you.

Episode 54

The Dog's Nose

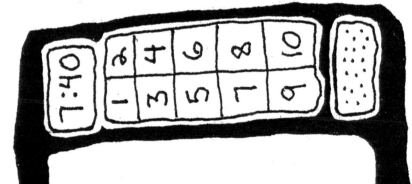

t's a slow afternoon and a small group of bartenders are hanging out at The Professor's bar, swapping cocktail recipes and discussing what's hot in the San Francisco bar scene.

"Seems to me that you can put anything you like in front of a customer just so long as you give it a weird name. It's a trend I wish would end," says Jen, a woman who tends bar at a nearby nightclub. "There's been a run on Slippery Nipples at our joint for the past month."

"Same happens here, Jen. One joker ordered a Slow Comfortable Screw Against The Wall with Satin Pillows yesterday," The Professor tells her.

"What the heck's that?"

"Not a clue, Jen. Not a clue. Fact is, though, strange or suggestive drink names aren't just a current trend—the Bosom Caresser's been around since the late 1800s. The Brain Duster, too. And how about the Dog's Nose? That one goes back even further. Not a bad drink, either."

The Dog's Nose dates back to the early nineteenth century. It is a very strange drink that's made with hot stout, gin, sugar, and nutmeg. Since stout, such as Guinness, is a robust beer, a stout-hearted gin must be employed in the Dog's Nose to make sure that the gin doesn't get lost in the drink. Junipero, made in San Francisco, is a good choice, and Beefeater, Boodles, Plymouth, and Tanqueray gins work well here, too. There's also a very good new gin on the market, Miller's Westbourne, that's ideal for making the Dog's Nose. Softer styles of gin, such as Bombay, Hendrick's, and Tanqueray No. TEN, however, are best reserved for use in fruitier drinks, such as the Bronx Cocktail, the Ramos Gin Fizz, and Cosmopolitans made with gin instead of vodka—a variation that's well worth a try.

"Okay, Professor, spill it. What's a Dog's Nose?" asks Jen.

"Ever read *Pickwick Papers*?"

"Can't say that I have."

"Well, if you ever get around to it you'll read about a certain Mr. Walker, who blamed his love of the Dog's Nose for the loss of the use of his right hand." The Professor clears his throat and quotes the book, "'if he had drunk nothing but water all his life, his fellow-workman would never have stuck a rusty

needle in him, and thereby occasioned the accident.' Wanna risk one, Jen?"

"Bring it on, Professor."

The Professor assembles the drink and sends it back to the kitchen where the Leo, the chef, heats it in the microwave and brings the glass back to the bar.

"What the heck is this anyway, Professor?" asks Leo.

"Dog's Nose, chef. And don't ask me why it's called Dog's Nose. I haven't the foggiest." Leo studies The Professor for a couple of seconds.

"Stick your finger in the drink, Professor," the chef says. The Professor complies.

"Pretty wet, huh? Now tell me what color it is."

"It's, well, I guess it's black. What's your point?"

"Never mind, Professor. Just let me know if you ever figure out how the drink got its name. You know where to find me."

The Dog's Nose

160 ml (2 oz) Guinness
2 teaspoons brown sugar
60 ml (2 oz) gin
Freshly grated nutmeg, as garnish
Pour the Guinness into a large sturdy glass and heat it in a microwave for about 1 minute. Add the brown sugar and gin and stir lightly. Add the garnish.

A Word at the End of the Bar

The prose in *italics* in the piece above never made it into print. Slippery Nipples are not the kind of thing to mention in a family newspaper, but of course I wasn't thinking about that when I wrote it. I was thinking about slippery nipples. Here's what made it into the newspaper.

"Seems to me that you can put anything you like in front of a customer just so long as you give it a weird name. It's a trend I wish would end," says Jen, a woman who tends bar at a nearby nightclub. "There's been a run on Brass Monkeys at our joint for the past month."

"Same happens here, Jen. One joker ordered a Slow Comfortable Screw Against The Wall with Satin Pillows yesterday," The Professor tells her.

"What the heck's that?"

"Not a clue, Jen. Not a clue. Fact is, though, strange drink names aren't just a current trend—Blow My Skull Off has been around since the mid-1800s, and the Brain Duster dates to the turn of the twentieth century. And how about the Dog's Nose? That one goes back even further. Not a bad drink, either."

Episode 55

Jamaica Farewell

Bill, one of The Professor's childhood friends, is visiting San Francisco for a few days on business, and he and his bartender buddy are reminiscing about some of the adventures they shared a few decades ago.

"Remember when we rowed those people to shore from the floating island in Jamaica?"

"That's right," says Bill. "We saved them from the shoal of jellyfish and they bought us beer all afternoon."

"Let's drink to that," says The Professor. "Wanna try a Jamaica Farewell cocktail?"

"Sounds good to me."

The Jamaica Farewell is a drink created by Daniel Reichert, owner of Vintage Cocktails, a cocktail catering company in Los Angeles that provides drinks for events such as gallery openings, and private parties. It's made with rum, lime juice, bitters, and Apry, an apricot brandy liqueur made by Marie Brizard . Many fruit brandies are made from a neutral base, but this bottling is made with cognac and is flavored with apricots from France and South Africa. It's very rich, and very flavorful.

Reichert likes to use Appleton Estate VX rum as the base for the Jamaica Farewell, and this, too, is a very special spirit. Bacardi 8, a rich Puerto Rican rum, could be substituted here, as could the 8-year-old Rhum Barbancourt from Haiti, or Mount Gay, a rum made in Barbados. For the drink to be a true Jamaican Farewell, though, the Jamaican Appleton Estate VX is the rum of choice, and according to Reichert, Myers's, another Jamaican-made rum, doesn't work well in this drink.

The Professor pours the cocktails, the two old friends raise their glasses, and The Professor starts to sing "Jamaica Farewell," a song written by Irving Burgie a.k.a. Lord Burgess, in the 1950s.

> "Now I'm sad to say
> I'm on my way
> I won't be back for many a day
> My heart is down
> My head is turning around
> I had to leave a little girl in Kingston town."

Bill and The Professor smile large, clink glasses, and take a sip of their Jamaica Farewell cocktails. The door opens and Regina, the raunchy waitress, strides into the bar to start her shift.

"I could hear you guys singing half a block away," she scolds The Professor. "And you still can't hold a note to save your life. Good old song, though. Jimmy Buffett. *Songs You Know by Heart* album, right?"

"It might have been on that album, Regina, but Harry Belafonte recorded it first, way back in the fifties."

"So you remember it from your college days, huh, Professor?" Regina walks back toward the kitchen, chuckling.

"That woman sure knows how to push my buttons, Bill."

"She's just the person I need right now, then. Think she'll tell me how to push the one that'll get me another cocktail?"

The Professor shakes his head and starts to make the next round.

Jamaican Farewell

Adapted from a recipe by Daniel Reichert, Vintage Cocktails, Los Angeles.

60 ml (2 oz) Appleton Estate VX rum

22.5 ml (.75 oz) Marie Brizard Apry apricot brandy

22.5 ml (.75 oz) fresh lime juice

2 dashes Angostura bitters

1 lime wedge, as garnish

Fill a cocktail shaker two-thirds full of ice and add all of the ingredients. Shake for approximately 15 seconds and strain into a chilled cocktail glass. Add the garnish.

A Word at the End of the Bar

Okay, on this one occasion, The Professor was me. Bill Greenham has been my friend since we were five years old. We met on our first day of school, and we've been best of buddies ever since. Bill worked for the British Foreign Office back in the seventies, and I visited him on a couple of occasions when he was stationed in Jamaica. On my second trip to visit with Bill, Stan Ogden, a guy we met when he moved to our town at the age of eight, flew out to join us for a fabulous vacation in Discovery Bay. The three of us are as tight as thieves, though Bill and I have to keep reminding Stan that he's the newcomer.

Episode 56

The Aviation

"It cost Hughes nearly four million bucks to make *Hell's Angels* in 1930. The most expensive movie ever made until *Gone With the Wind* beat it nine years later. Not bad for a guy who dropped out of high school, huh?" Paul, the resident self-proclaimed movie buff at The Professor's bar, is holding forth on Howard Hughes' film career. The Professor is kicking himself for mentioning that he finally got around to seeing *The Aviator*, Martin Scorsese's flick starring Leonardo DiCaprio as the eccentric billionaire industrialist and Hollywood film mogul.

"I think he did have a little family money to fall back on, though, Paul," The Professor points out.

"Yeah, yeah, he was a poor little rich boy, but he sure knew how to live when he was young. Hollywood, airplanes, movie-star girlfriends . . ."

"Hypochondria," The Professor adds. "Fancy an Aviation Cocktail, Paul? You can toast your hero and discover an incredibly good old drink at the same time."

"Bring it on, Professor. Bring it on."

The Aviation dates back to the 1930s. It's a simple drink, calling for gin, maraschino liqueur, and fresh lemon juice, but it's the maraschino that makes this cocktail stand tall. Made from Dalmatian Marasca cherries, pits included, maraschino adds a little sweetness, and a wonderfully dry, peppery nuttiness to cocktails. There's a hint of cherries in the flavor profile, too. Many people who haven't tasted this liqueur are tempted to think that it could be as overly sweet as maraschino cherries are, but good maraschino liqueur, available under the Luxardo and Stock brand names, is far drier than the name might lead you to believe.

The Aviation might be the best known drink to employ maraschino, but The Floridita, basically a Daiquiri with a little maraschino added, is another incredibly good drink that owes much of its complexity to this liqueur.

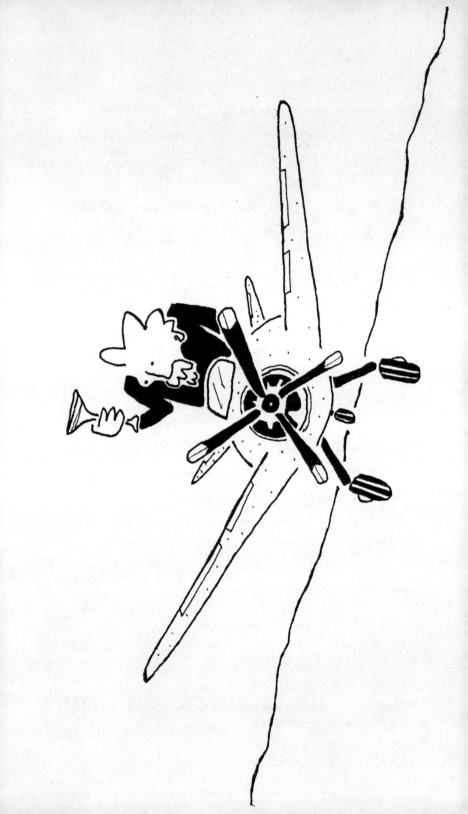

Doc, a frequent visitor to The Professor's bar, is sitting quietly at the mahogany reading *FDR: A Biography* by Ted Morgan. He looks up from his book and asks The Professor to fix him an Aviation Cocktail, too. The Professor prepares the drinks and sets them down in front of Paul and Doc.

"Got a toast for Howard Hughes?" The Professor asks the guys.

"This Ted Morgan guy once said something that might be appropriate," says Doc. He's a pretty astute biographer."

Doc raises his glass, and Paul follows suit, waiting for the toast. Doc speaks:

"Howard Hughes was able to afford the luxury of madness, like a man who not only thinks he is Napoleon but hires an army to prove it."

Paul looks a little puzzled. The Professor grins and walks down the bar.

The Aviation

60 ml (2 oz) gin
15 ml (.5 oz) maraschino liqueur
15 ml (.5 oz) fresh lemon juice
Fill a cocktail shaker two-thirds full of ice and add all of the
ingredients. Shake for approximately 15 seconds. Strain into
a chilled cocktail glass.

A Word at the End of the Bar

I got a lot wrong in this column, huh? This was written before Dave Wondrich found the original recipe for the Aviation in *Recipes for Mixed Drinks* by Hugo Ensslin, 1916. I think I'm right in saying that I, along with a lot of other cocktail geeks, thought at the time that the drink had first seen the light of day in *The Savoy Cocktail Book*, 1930. The recipe from the *Savoy* didn't call for crème de violette, and even if it did, when this column was printed we couldn't get our hands on crème de violette in the U.S.A., so that ingredient would have been superfluous at the time. Now, though, things have changed. Wondrich has become my personal researcher and I steal from him on a very regular basis, and crème de violette is pretty readily available these days, so here's another recipe for you.

Aviation

45 ml (1.5 oz) gin
15 ml (.5 oz) maraschino liqueur
15 ml (.5 oz) crème de violette
15 ml (.5 oz) fresh lemon juice
Shake over ice and strain into a chilled cocktail glass.

Index

X

Z

Printed by BoD™in Norderstedt, Germany